THE
MYSTERIES
OF
TROY

THE MYSTERIES OF TROY

I. G. Edmonds

THOMAS NELSON INC., PUBLISHERS

Nashville   New York

Copyright © 1977 by I. G. Edmonds

First edition

Library of Congress Cataloging in Publication Data

Edmonds, I G
    The mysteries of Troy.

    Bibliography: p. 183
    Includes index.
    SUMMARY: Discusses the history, literature and legends, archaeology, and art of this ancient Turkish city, scene of much of Homer's "Iliad" and "Odyssey."
    1. Troy—Juvenile literature. [1. Troy.   2. Cities and towns, Ancient]   I. Title.
DF221.T8E3   939.2'1   77-1058
ISBN 0-8407-6533-9

ACKNOWLEDGMENTS

Line drawings and engravings reproduced are from Schliemann's *Ilios: The City and Country of the Trojans*, 1880.

All photographs of the ruins are by the author.

Quotations attributed to Heinrich Schliemann are from his autobiography, published as an introduction to his book *Ilios*.

Quotations from the *Iliad* are based upon the translation of Andrew Lang, Walter Leaf, and Ernest Myers, published by Macmillan in 1882. In some quotes the original translations are modified to remove archaic phrases and to improve clarity.

CONTENTS

This engraving from *Ilios*, the book Schliemann published in 1880, shows Sophia (only a fair likeness) wearing the famed diadem of Troy.

THE
MYSTERIES
OF
TROY

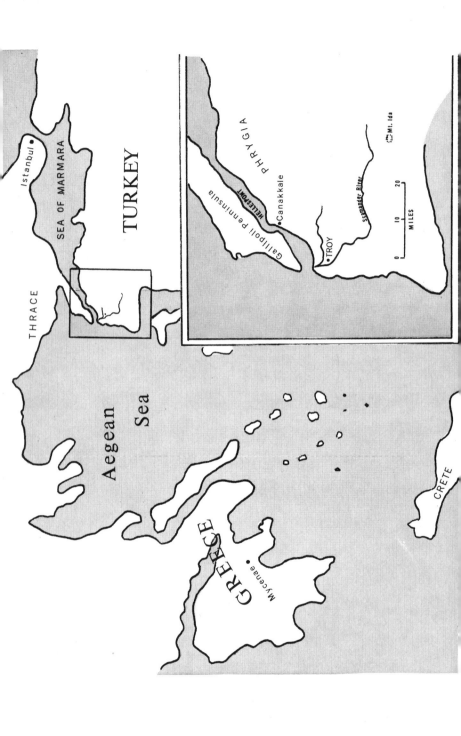

INTRODUCTION:
THE SILENT STONES

She stood atop the ruins of a rock wall, looking across the Troad toward the Dardanelles four miles away. She could not have been far from the spot where Homer tells us that Helen of Troy stood when King Priam asked her to look at the battlefield and to identify for him the Greek leaders who were attacking Troy.

The modern girl on the ancient wall hardly resembled the famous Helen whose face—so we are told—launched a thousand ships. This girl was in her teens. She wore faded jeans and had a knapsack on her back. She was obviously one of the many European students who buy a train pass and roam about the continent during their summer vacations.

She turned as I came up, stumbling over stones shaped by an unknown people almost five thousand years ago. She smiled, and I took the opportunity to ask what she thought of the ruins. Her English was somewhat imperfect, and she did not entirely understand my question. She thought I had asked what she was thinking.

She replied, "I am thinking that I would like to squeeze each rock until it was forced to tell me what really happened here!"

Her emotions are shared by most visitors who come to see the nine levels of Troy, the city of Homer, which archaeologists have

11

uncovered in the mound at Hissarlik, a town on the Turkish coast just below where the Dardanelles (the ancient Hellespont) joins the Sea of Marmara and the Aegean Sea.

Troy is one of the famous cities of history. The story of how Paris, prince of Troy, stole Helen, wife of Menelaus of Sparta, and caused the vengeful Greeks to launch a ten-year war against the Trojans is known throughout the world. In grade school we read simplified versions of how the Greeks tricked the people of Troy by hiding inside the famous Wooden Horse. Later in high school we studied Homer's *Iliad*, the story of Achilles' wrath and the tragedy it brought to the Greeks at Troy. We then read the *Odyssey*, recounting the fall of Troy and the trials of Odysseus in returning home.

Homer's epic poems recount only a brief segment of the fascinating story of a city that had nine lives, stretching from 3000 B.C. to A.D. 400. Some of the most famous names in history have been enthralled by Troy's story and have speculated, studied, and searched for the truth about the city.

Despite all that has been learned of Troy in 2,500 years of study and research, the silent stones of the ruined city still hold many unexplained mysteries, which hide secrets of history, literature, archaeology, and art. In a lesser way the secrets of Troy could shed light on the origin of Greek mythology and give us valuable information about the change from the Stone Age to the Bronze Age. They might also shed light on the original settlement of Greece, the mysterious origin of the great Mycenaean empire and the bull-worshiping people of Crete, the rise of the Hittites in Anatolia, and dozens of other historical mysteries.

Students of literature have their own questions to ask the silent rocks of Troy. This is because Homer's epics, which are the bedrock of the Trojan legend, mark the beginning of written Greek literature. Homer's influence upon both Greek and Western culture is enormous. A steady stream of the greatest writers from classical Greece to modern times have drawn inspiration from Homer.

In ancient Greece Aeschylus, Sophocles, and Euripides all based tragic plays upon the Trojan legends. In Roman times Vergil's epic *Aeneid*, Ovid's poetry, and Seutonius' *Life of Julius Caesar* are part of a mass of work that kept the spirit of Troy alive. According to Seutonius, Caesar, who traced his ancestry to Troy, once considered moving the capital of the Roman Empire to Troy.

In the Middle Ages Chaucer, Boccaccio, and John Lydgate used Trojan subjects in their writings. Dante made allusions to Troy in *The Divine Comedy*. Later William Shakespeare, John Milton, and Christopher Marlowe wrote of Troy. In fact, it was Marlowe who wrote the famous lines quoted so often about Helen of Troy:

> Was this the face that launch'd a thousand ships,
> And burnt the topless towers of Ilium?

Incidentally, Marlow—and Shakespeare after him—stole the line about the "face that launch'd a thousand ships" from Lucian of Samostata, a Greek satirist of the second century A.D.

Later writers who found inspiration in Troy include Edgar Allan Poe, Goethe, Lord Byron, Samuel Butler—and into modern times—Gabriele d'Annunzio, John Masefield, James Joyce, Robert Graves, and Stephen Vincent Benét. Eugene O'Neill used an offshoot of the Trojan legend, the tragedy of Agamemnon, as the source of his famous trilogy, *Mourning Becomes Electra*.

Troy has been an equally fruitful source of inspiration for artists for the past three thousand years. We first find Trojan scenes from the *Iliad* on Greek vases. They also turned up on Greek and Roman coins and in statuary like the famous Laocoön group of a father and sons struggling with a serpent sent to kill them for warning the Trojans that the Wooden Horse was a Greek trick. The expression, "Beware of Greeks bearing gifts!" is Vergil's paraphrase of Laocoön's warning.

The excavated walls of long-buried Pompeii revealed many mosaics and frescoes based upon Trojan scenes. In succeeding years the great masters added their contributions. These included Cranach, Raphael, El Greco, Brueghel the Elder, Rubens, Van Dyck, Lorrain, Watteau, Reynolds, Wedgwood (ceramics), Benjamin West, Daumier, Rodin (sculpture), Renoir, and Sargent, among many others.

Romantic and exciting as Troy's past is, even in modern times the city produced a new legend in Heinrich Schliemann, who rediscovered the lost ruins. Schliemann's life is like something from Horatio Alger's fiction. He was a penniless boy who became a millionaire through hard work. At the peak of success he quit and devoted his life and fortune to the search for Troy. In the end he found not only the ancient city, but buried treasure and his own personal Helen of Troy. In all history no person has ever had an extravagant dream come true as completely as Heinrich Schliemann did.

But despite years of digging by archaeologists, not all of Troy has yet been excavated. Even more important, there are other mounds and tumuli in the Troad that have not been thoroughly investigated. Tradition assigns the graves of Hector, Achilles, and Patroclus to this area, but excavations of tumuli said to be their graves produced no sign of burial or cremation. Perhaps, like the famous treasure Schliemann found, their treasures continue to lie with their ashes in a still-undiscovered location.

This treasure might even include the fabulous shield that the armorer of the gods forged in Olympus for Achilles. The dream of finding this shield is no more fantastic than what really happened when Schliemann uncovered the golden diadems of a lost queen of Troy and the mysterious golden masks of the Mycenaean kings.

The mysteries of the Trojan ruins are conducive to such dreams, for Troy is a place where dreams can come true. Heinrich Schliemann proved that with a definiteness that cannot be denied.

1

THE SEARCH FOR TROY

The Reverend Ernest Schliemann, a Protestant pastor in a small German town, felt that the usual children's stories were frivolous. He preferred to tell his children tales from the great classics, recasting the stories in simple language. The story his six-year-old son Heinrich loved best was the *Iliad*, the epic tale of Troy related by the Greek poet Homer.

The boy listened in open-mouthed wonder as his father told how Agamemnon, leader of the Greeks besieging Troy, offended Achilles, mightiest of the Greek warriors. Achilles then withdrew from battle, almost causing the Greeks to lose the war. The characters in the *Iliad* are so finely drawn that they come alive to the reader, and Pastor Schliemann, a born storyteller, was able to carry over Homer's characterizations in his recounting of the epic poem. The story made such an impression on young Heinrich that his future life was molded by what he heard.

Years later he wrote:

My father always found me a warm defender of the Trojan cause. With great grief I heard from him that Troy had been so completely destroyed that it had disappeared without leaving any traces of its existence. My joy may be imagined when, being nearly eight years old, I received, in 1829, as a Christmas gift, Dr. Georg Ludwig Jerrer's *Universal History*. It contained an engraving representing Troy in flames, with its huge walls and the Scaean gate, from which Aeneas is escaping.

I cried out, "Father, you are mistaken. Jerrer must have seen Troy, otherwise he could not have presented it here."

"My son," he replied. "That is merely a fanciful picture."

"Father," I said, "if such walls once existed, they cannot possibly have been completely destroyed. Vast ruins must still remain, but hidden beneath the dust of ages."

Pastor Schliemann disagreed but was amused by his son's enthusiasm. The ruins of Pompeii in Italy were still being excavated at this time, and both father and son took a great interest in the discoveries made there. Heinrich began to dream of similarly uncovering the ruins of his beloved Troy. Though the elder Schliemann had no faith in this, he indulgently agreed that when Heinrich was grown, he should go look for the site of Homer's city.

Writing as an old man, Schliemann said that all his playmates except one laughed at his enthusiasm for Troy. The one who believed in him was Minna Meincke, daughter of a farmer who lived nearby. She was the same age as Heinrich. Schliemann wrote, "Minna entered into all my vast plans for the future. Thus a warm attachment grew up between us. In our childish simplicity we exchanged vows of eternal love."

From the time he was nine years old, Heinrich Schliemann planned his entire life around Minna. They would marry when they were grown. Then they would excavate a grim castle near their homes where a famous robber baron, Henning von Holstein, was said to have buried a great treasure. The money from this find would be used by them to sail for Asia Minor, where they would excavate Troy and find a still greater treasure.

Alas for his dreams. Heinrich's mother died and his father took the housemaid to live with him. The outraged townspeople turned against the entire Schliemann family. Minna was forbidden to see Heinrich again.

"In later life," Schliemann wrote, "I have undergone many troubles in different parts of the world, but none of them ever caused me a thousandth part of the grief I felt at the age of nine years for my separation from my little bride."

Heinrich was sent to live with an uncle in a nearby town. Then, when he was fourteen, he was apprenticed to a local grocer. For the next five and a half years the boy literally slaved without salary. He retained only one pleasant memory of those years. This was of an alcoholic miller who could recite the *Iliad* from memory in the original Greek. Schliemann could not understand a word of it, but he was fascinated by the rhythm of the epic poem that the drunken man recited.

Shortly after his twentieth birthday Schliemann strained himself lifting a barrel of potato whiskey. Unable to do hard work anymore, he went to Hamburg, where he found and lost two jobs because he was not strong enough to do the work. Finally, in desperation, he signed on as a ship's cabin boy. His bad luck held. He was shipwrecked in a heavy storm off the coast of Holland.

Germany held only bitter memories for the young man, so he decided to remain in Holland. For the next three years he worked in Amsterdam, earning about $160 a year. He tells us, "My lodging was a wretched garret without a fire, where I shivered in the winter and was scorched with heat in the summer. My breakfast consisted of rye-meal porridge and my dinner never cost more than two-pence."

During these bitter years, Schliemann spent his spare time learning languages. He developed his own method of study. He obtained a copy of Sir Walter Scott's *Ivanhoe* and an English dictionary. With the help of the dictionary, he read *Ivanhoe* every night. Then on Sunday he went to an English church in Amsterdam. He sat in the back and silently repeated each word of the minister's sermon to get the correct accent and pronunciation of the words he had learned from *Ivanhoe* and the dictionary. He developed a phenomenal memory. In time he memorized both *Ivanhoe* and Oliver Goldsmith's *The Vicar of Wakefield*.

After learning English and, of course, Dutch, Schliemann turned to French. Later he learned Spanish, Portuguese, and Italian.

This working knowledge of six foreign languages obtained him a position with an important import-export firm. His new salary was double his old one. It was doubled again when his new employers discovered how hard he worked.

Schliemann's years of destitution were now over forever. He was twenty-three years old. He soon saw that his company had a genuine need for someone who could speak Russian to help with its large branch office in St. Petersburg. Schliemann quickly learned the language, and in 1846 his employers, B. H. Schroder and Company, sent him to Russia as their agent.

Schliemann did enormously well from the first. He increased Schroder's business and branched off for himself by trading in indigo dye imported from India.

Now on the road to success, Schliemann wrote to a friend in Germany, whom he asked to present his proposal of marriage to Minna. A month later the answer came back that she had recently married a local farmer.

"I considered this disappointment at the time to be the greatest disaster which could befall me. I was for some time utterly unfit for any occupation and sick in bed," Schliemann said. "I constantly recalled to mind all that had passed between Minna and myself in early childhood, all our sweet dreams and plans."

Schliemann now lived only for his work. By 1850 he was worth $40,000, a large sum for that day. Then he received word that his younger brother, Louis, had died in San Francisco, leaving a considerable fortune made in the 1849 California gold rush. Schliemann closed his Russian business and went to California. He found that Louis's partner had absconded with all the gold. Schliemann then took his $40,000 and settled down to banking and buying gold dust from miners.

While he was in San Francisco, the Territory of California became a state, and foreigners then residing there had the privilege of becoming naturalized citizens. Schliemann accepted, but left the state in 1852, after doubling his money. He resumed his business in Russia, married a cold Russian woman who hated him, and finally, in 1863, retired a millionaire at the age of forty-one.

He spent the next few years traveling alone through the world and managing some business properties he retained. "But," he wrote, "I never forgot Troy, or the agreement I had made with my father and Minna to excavate it."

Eventually Schliemann's wanderings took him to Ithaca, the rocky island off the west coast of Greece that is the legendary home of Odysseus. From Ithaca Schliemann went to the ruins of Mycenae, home of Agamemnon, who led the Greek forces in the Trojan war. Mycenae is below Corinth on the Argolic Peninsula. It is situated on a high hill overlooking the Plain of Argos.

Leaving Mycenae, Schliemann went in search of Troy. The Troad—the Plain of Troy—is on the west coast of Turkey at the point where the strait of Dardanelles opens into the Aegean Sea.

The site of Troy had long since been forgotten. Most archaeologists and historians of Schliemann's time no longer believed that there had ever been a real Troy. Many denied that there had ever been a Homer, claiming that the *Iliad* and the *Odyssey* were compilations of songs made by poets over a long period of time. The few who still insisted that Troy had existed believed the site to be at Bunarbashi, a hill located about eight miles from the Aegean coast.

Schliemann looked upon Homer as gospel. If something was written in the *Iliad*, then in his mind it was fact. He went to Bunarbashi, in his hand a copy of the *Iliad* with every geographical reference marked. Homer said that Mount Ida was visible in a certain direction from Troy. Schliemann could not see Mount Ida from Bunarbashi. He did not question Homer. He questioned those who declared that this place was the probable site of ancient Troy.

Again Homer said that Achilles the Greek pursued Hector the Trojan three times around the walls of Troy. Schliemann walked around the Bunarbashi site. He found a steep drop on one side.

"I had to crawl backward on all fours," he reported. "I carried away the conviction that no mortal being, not even a goat, has ever been able to run swiftly down a slope that descends at an angle of 25 degrees."

Poring over his well-worn copy of the *Iliad*, Schliemann used Homer's account of travels between the sea and the city to figure the possible distance of Troy from the water. He decided that it had to be from three to four miles. Bunarbashi was eight.

Convinced now that Bunarbashi could not possibly be the site of Homer's Troy, Schliemann turned to other sites in the Troad. An odd-shaped mound on an outcropping near the village of Hissarlik next engaged his interest. *Hissarlik* means "fortress," and the village drew its name from the curious shape of the mound, which, from a distance, gave the impression of a citadel.

Hissarlik fit all the geographical requirements of Homer. Mount Ida was visible in the right direction. The rivers were in the right place. And the site was three miles from the Dardanelles and four miles from the Aegean seacoast. Equally important, Hector and Achilles could have run around the site.

Schliemann found that others before him had considered Hissarlik as the possible site of Troy. In 1822—the year of Schliemann's birth—Charles Maclaren of Edinburgh, Scotland, published a book called *The Topography of Troy*, based upon his visit to the Troad in 1820. Maclaren said that *if* there had ever been a real Troy, it would have been at Hissarlik.

Frank Calvert, brother of an Englishman who acted as American vice consul at Canakkale, a town six miles from the site, also believed Hissarlik to be Troy. Calvert owned half of the Hissarlik site. Two Turks owned the remainder. Calvert welcomed Schliemann and showed him around the mound. Calvert had dug two small ditches himself, uncovering some Roman artifacts. Calvert also pointed out to Schliemann that the famous Wooden Horse that figured in the fall of Troy could not possibly have been dragged from the sea to Bunarbashi, but could have been brought to Hissarlik.

Schliemann was convinced, and he was eager to prove the theory by digging in the mound. However, he realized his lack of technical knowledge. He left the Troad and went to Paris, where he spent two years studying archaeology. He also wrote a book, *Ithaque, le Peloponnese et Troie*, which he published at his own expense. Curiously, he wrote the book in English, and then had it translated into French and his native German. In it he described the ruins of

The Troad, or Plain of Troy, looking from the southwest walls of Troy VI toward the Aegean Sea beyond the low hills in the distance.

Ithaca, Mycenae, and Troy. The book earned him a doctor of philosophy degree from the Rostock University in Germany. Schliemann was very proud of this academic honor, and ever after he was hurt if distinguished people failed to refer to him as Dr. Schliemann.

Schliemann was a small man. He looked more like a clerk than like a millionaire businessman. He was intolerant of those who opposed him and became angry when he could not get his way. His feelings were easily hurt also and he was very sentimental. He never forgot his childhood sweetheart, Minna, and once broke into tears at the death of a female cousin.

Schliemann announced that he intended to excavate the Hissarlik mound, but first he went to the United States, where he was still a citizen through his California naturalization, and applied for a divorce from his Russian wife. He settled in Indianapolis, Indiana, because friends assured him a divorce would easily be attained there. However, it took a full year, and Schliemann occupied his time in business.

When the decree was finally granted, he wrote to a friend in Greece, requesting help in finding a Greek wife. He gave precise instructions. She must be young and an orphan. He preferred a cultured woman who had been a governess to children. But most important of all, she absolutely had to love Homer.

Two months later he received a package of photographs from Greece. They were all lovely girls, but one stood out above all the others in his eyes, seventeen-year-old Sophia Engastromenos. She was neither an orphan nor a governess, but since she looked like Schliemann's conception of Helen of Troy, he was willing to overlook some of his requirements.

He went to Athens to meet her and was captivated. But his courtship was strange indeed. He did not tell her how lovely she was or bring her pretty presents in the manner of lovers. Instead he gave her examinations on the *Iliad* and the *Odyssey*. Rather than walking hand in hand in the moonlight, Sophia answered such questions as the name of the girl whom Agamemnon and Achilles quarrelled over, and whose idea it had been to build the famed Trojan Horse. Fortunately, Sophia did know her Homer, and the romance blossomed.

However, the romance faltered when Schliemann asked why she wanted to marry him. She replied that her parents said that he was rich. Schliemann was offended. He thought that she was interested in his money instead of himself, although he had done precious little to make any girl admire him for himself alone. He wrote her a little note in which he said he was going away, but that she would always remain in his heart as a true friend.

Sophia wrote back immediately. She said she had spoken as she thought a young girl should, for it was improper for her to speak of affection. Schliemann swallowed his pride, and they were married at a Greek wedding in Athens.

After spending a year in Paris, Schliemann took his bride to Hissarlik in 1871. He was determined to prove his theory that the ruins of Troy still existed. He wrote later that Sophia joined him with enthusiasm, "executing the great work upon which, nearly half a century ago, my childish simplicity had agreed upon with my father and planned with Minna." Although he was supremely happy with his young Greek wife, Schliemann never forgot Minna and spoke of her to the day he died.

Schliemann, playing upon his American citizenship, got the American ambassador in Istanbul to help him obtain a *firman* (an official permission) to dig at Hissarlik. The firman required that any archaeological treasures found must be divided with the Turkish government for the national museum in the capital.

The excavations began in September, 1871. Schliemann employed seventy native diggers, who worked with picks, wooden shovels, baskets, and eight wheelbarrows. They laboriously dug shafts into the hardened clay, carried the loose material out of the hole in baskets, and dumped it into the wheelbarrows to be carried away. Scientific archaeology was still in the future. Digging up the past still consisted of little more than searching for antique treasures to grace museums and private collections. The laborers received the equivalent of about thirty cents a day for their work. This was more than they could make as farm laborers, so they were pleased to work, but they often became disgruntled at their employer's impatience.

Six and a half feet down they struck the foundations of a Greek-period senate building. Schliemann, interested in nothing except Homer's Troy, had the stones pried up and continued digging. They next uncovered some massive stones that undoubtedly came from a fortified wall. At twenty feet he found burned earth and sun-dried bricks that had been scorched in some great fire. Excited now, for the burned area suggested Homer's Troy, which had been burned by the vengeful Greeks, Schliemann decided to dig a deep trench completely across the mound.

The severe Turkish winter brought the excavation to a halt, but Schliemann and Sophia went back to the site in March, 1872. The impatient German increased his work force to 150 laborers in answer to critics who scoffed at his claim that Troy was at Hissarlik.

As work progressed, Schliemann confided to Sophia his belief that they would find the treasure of King Priam. He had no authority in Homer or later Greek tradition to support such a belief. On the contrary, Homer implied that the Greeks had looted and burned the city. Schliemann, for once, refused to accept Homer. All his life Schliemann had been dazzled by the thought of buried treasure. As a poor boy in his native German village he had dreamed of finding the treasure hidden by the robber baron Holstein, which, he had told Minna, would finance their excavations of Troy so that they could find the still greater treasure of King Priam. In the passing years Priam's treasure had become an obsession with him. Now that he was on the site of Troy he refused to believe that no treasure existed.

In his eagerness to find the treasure, Schliemann destroyed everything that got in his way. He uncovered the foundation of a beautiful temple to Athena, Greek goddess of wisdom. He dug on through it. He next uncovered the massive walls of what later proved to be Troy VI. He ordered the stones broken out of place so that the trench could be deepened.

Ilhan Aksit, archaeologist for the Trojan museum in Canakkale, calls Schliemann a "butcher" because of this clumsy ruthlessness.

"His [Schliemann's] sin of destroying the magnificent temple of Athena will certainly outweigh a thousandfold the merit he gained by discovering Troy," Aksit wrote.

Although the temple was more than two thousand years old, it was modern to Schliemann, who only sought "sacred Ilium." How-

This is part of the great ditch that Schliemann dug across the ruins, exposing the first level of Troy.

ever, in his autobiography (appendix to his book *Ilios*), he showed a tinge of conscience by noting, "It was necessary to remove earlier antiquities in order to expose the true Troy."

As the trench was deepened, new surprises awaited Schliemann. The excavations kept revealing additional layers made by destroyed cities, each built upon the leveled ruins of the previous one. Finally Schliemann came to the walls of what was later identified as Troy II. These walls were extremely well built, but exploratory shafts showed that excavators had not yet reached bedrock. Schliemann was convinced that Homer's Troy was the first city built on the site. He gave orders to remove these new walls and dig on to bedrock.

The picks of his laborers finally hit bedrock fifty-three feet below the top surface of the Hissarlik mound. The first Troy was finally revealed, but it was a bitter disappointment. It was not the grandiose citadel his dreams had pictured from reading the *Iliad*. The place had definitely been a city and not just a Neolithic village, but it was certainly nothing like the "wide-wayed" city Homer described.

Schliemann refused to accept arguments that Homer had exaggerated. He pointed out that this could not be Homer's city because no copper objects were found in the debris. It was plainly a Stone Age settlement. All accounts of the Trojan War placed it in the Bronze Age.

Schliemann also found cracks in the remaining walls and foundations of Troy I. This indicated that the city had been destroyed by an earthquake. He turned back for a closer inspection of Troy II, which he mistakenly called Troy III due to his failure to identify properly the two layers of Troy I. Troy II was built upon a foundation of three feet of Troy I debris.

Troy II was fifty-three feet above the Trojan plain. It clearly showed a much improved culture. More important to Schliemann, this city had definitely been burned. There were extensive layers of ashes and some of the sun-dried bricks had been fused into rude glass by their exposure to intense heat.

Schliemann was certain that this was Homer's Troy. Everything—in his view—pointed to it. Troy I now fitted into the picture he envisioned. Troy, according to legend, had been destroyed in Priam's father's day by Poseidon, god of the sea, who was also thought to be responsible for earthquakes. Poseidon shook down the Trojan walls so that Heracles could sack the city after Laomedon, Priam's father, refused to pay a debt to the Greek strongman.

Schliemann was jubilant, but it was too late in the season to continue digging. He and Sophia went back to Athens.

They returned to Hissarlik in February 1873. Schliemann soon had 160 laborers removing dirt and debris. Discovery after discovery was unearthed. The first was the stone foundation—about six feet high—of what later proved to be part of the main gate of Troy VI. Schliemann called it the Great Tower of Ilium. In another location they found huge pottery jars as tall as a man. Next they uncovered a portion of paved road. Schliemann, as usual, gave these only momentary interest. All his efforts were devoted to uncovering Troy II, where he expected to find Priam's hidden treasure. Rereading Homer, he found no reference to any of the Greek loot being identified as belonging to Priam. Thus he figured that the royal treasures had been buried before the fall of the city.

Suddenly the work came to a stunning climax. Schliemann never revealed the exact date, but it was sometime in late May or early June of 1873. It was his policy to have the workmen out at dawn. The thirty cents a day he paid them was a generous wage, and he expected the men to earn it. They worked until eight o'clock, when there was a rest period and a breakfast provided by Schliemann.

He and Sophia were inspecting the dig about an hour before the breakfast hour. Suddenly Schliemann's eye was caught by the glint of copper in the sun. A workman's pick had cut through the oxides on the side of a buried copper jug. The imprisoning dirt had fallen away from one side of the jug, which was embedded in the side of a deep shaft. Behind the jug Schliemann thought he glimpsed the glint of gold, which does not corrode. Anything that bright could be nothing but the precious metal.

Shaking with excitement, he jumped down into the shaft. The walls were insecure, and there was danger of their collapsing on him, but he paid no attention to the danger as he dug out the copper jar with a pocketknife. Almost choking with emotion, he called to Sophia, directing her to order the workmen to take a rest. None were digging at the moment in this particular hole, but Schliemann did not want them to see what he was doing. She passed the order to the surprised foreman, who ordered the diggers from the pits.

In Schliemann's words:

> While the men were resting and eating, I cut out the Treasure with a large knife. This required great exertion and involved great risk, since the wall of the fortification beneath which I had to dig threatened every moment to fall down on me. But the sight of so many objects, every one of which is of inestimable value to archaeology, made me reckless. I never thought of any danger.

His teenage wife was equally oblivious to the danger of being buried alive. Clutching her ankle-long skirts, she lowered herself into the pit with her husband. The treasure turned out to be larger than Schliemann had dreamed. As he pulled golden earrings, necklaces, pots of silver and gold, and other priceless objects from the cache, Sophia carefully placed them on her spread shawl.

The most important of the find were two golden diadems. They were alike, except that one was larger than the other. This suggests that one had been worn by a queen and the other by a princess. The first diadem was a band of thin gold that circled the wearer's head. Tiny gold rings were attached to the circle. Suspended from the rings were gold wires covered with golden leaves that made short bangs across the wearer's face and hung to the shoulders on each side of the face. At the bottom of the strings of leaves, attached to the wires, were tiny replicas of some curious stone images later found at Troy.

The second diadem was similar in design.

Mrs. Schliemann smuggled the treasure back to their home. They were being secretive because half of the treasure rightfully belonged to the Turkish government. Behind drawn shades Schliemann reverently inspected each piece. He took one of the diadems and placed it around Sophia's head. Tears came to his eyes. He whispered huskily, "My Helena!"

Sophia Schliemann wearing the "treasure of Priam," including the famous diadem, necklace, and earrings. Photo by Schuchhardt, *Schliemann's Excavations*, 1891.

No daydreaming boy ever had his dream come so completely true as Heinrich Schliemann. He had dreamed of finding Troy, and he had found it. He had dreamed of finding treasure, and he had found it too. And along with it he had found his own personal Helen of Troy.

Schliemann's great concern was to get the treasure out of Turkey before officials discovered that he had it. He hid the gold and silver at Frank Calvert's home for two days and then secretly took it to a ship for transport to Greece. He quickly closed the dig; then he and Sophia went to Greece, where they retrieved the treasure. From there Schliemann took it to Germany.

The secret leaked out in January 1874, when the Turkish police caught two of Schliemann's former diggers with golden objects the German had overlooked. The Turks realized then that Schliemann had gotten away with a greater treasure. They demanded its return. Schliemann ignored their claims. The Turks then sued Schliemann in the Greek courts and won a $5,000 judgment. At this time only Schliemann and Sophia knew how rich the treasure was.

Schliemann announced that he would not pay, claiming the articles he found were not worth $5,000. He said he would not return to Troy, and began digging in Mycenae on the Greek plain of Argos, the home of Agamemnon, leader of the Greek forces that had stormed Troy. He hoped to find a new treasure here. However, the call of Troy was too much for him. Working through the good offices of both the American ambassador and the German ambassador in Istanbul, he agreed to pay the fine in exchange for new permission to dig again at Hissarlik. When the firman was granted, Schliemann surprised everyone by giving the Turkish government five times the fine, or $25,000. The firman required Schliemann to give the Turkish Museum first pick of all future finds at Troy, and officials were appointed to watch him and make sure that he kept this part of the bargain.

No one denied that Schliemann had found an ancient city, but few historians and archaeologists would agree that he had found Homer's Troy. Many still insisted that Troy was a literary myth.

Even those who believed in a real Troy could not reconcile their beliefs with what Schliemann had found. The Troy of Schliemann, even allowing for poetic license, was a far cry from the glorious city that Homer had sung of.

Angry and hurt, Schliemann struck back at his detractors. Always impatient with anyone who opposed him, he had grown more intolerant as he aged. He kept insisting that he had indeed found Homer's Troy, and he rejected every argument against it.

But in this he was wrong. He had found the *site* of Homer's Troy, the "sacred Ilium" of his dreams, but not the actual city. In his greed to find Priam's treasure, Schliemann had dug right through the city he sought and ended up seventeen hundred years further into the remote past.

The bedrock city of Troy I was founded about 3000 B.C. Troy II, the city Schliemann thought was Ilium, was built about 2500 B.C. The Troy of Achilles, Priam, Paris, Hector, Odysseus, and the eternally lovely Helen is now believed to have been Troy VII-a, which lasted only one hundred years, from about 1300 to about 1200 B.C.

2

THE FIRST TROYS

Three thousand B.C.—give or take a couple of hundred years on either side of the date, since dating prehistory is still an inexact science—was a turning point in human history. Civilization was on the march. The Sumerians in the Tigris and Euphrates valleys and the Egyptians along the Nile had developed the first systems of writing. Also in Egypt Pharaoh Menes had united the upper and lower kingdoms of the Nile to create the First Dynasty. The beginning of civilization along the Yellow River in China was only two hundred years in the future. The Sphinx and the Great Pyramid were still five hundred years in the future.

While civilization was emerging in Egypt and along the Tigris and Euphrates rivers in Mesopotamia, Stone Age men still roamed through most of Europe. The Lake Dwellers were building homes on pilings driven into the waters of Switzerland. And a people called the Danubians for want of a better name had crossed from Asia Minor and were sweeping up the Danube River in a great migration that would take them all the way to the North Sea.

At the time that these Stone Age people were restlessly migrating across Europe and Asia, the late Stone Age was drawing to a close elsewhere as inquisitive men learned to use copper and then how to harden it with tin to make bronze.

During the great migrations around 3000 B.C. an unknown people built a small city on an outcropping of rock that rose forty-eight feet above what became known as the plain of Troy. There are absolutely no historical clues as to where they came from. Nothing is known about the color of their skin or their physical features. We know nothing of their language or how they dressed. We don't even know what became of them after a disastrous earthquake leveled their stone and mud-brick dwellings. They are an almost complete historical mystery.

There is considerable information about how they lived. The excavations of Schliemann and, later, Wilhelm Dörpfeld and Carl Blegen show that the first Troy was a true city. It was apparently the capital of a district. Other excavations have revealed smaller settlements in the area. However, they were not fortified, and Troy was.

The original Trojan wall was built of rough rock set in a herringbone pattern, which is not found in any of the other eight levels. The base of the wall was broad and tapered toward the top. Since the crudeness of the stone dressing and the batter (meaning that the wall sloped, instead of being perpendicular) would make the walls easy to scale by an enemy, archaeologists have surmised that a straight wall, or parapet, of sun-dried bricks sat atop the slanting stone wall.

There was a gate in the south wall. It was almost six feet wide and was protected by a tower from which Trojan soldiers could shoot arrows and drop stone missiles down upon an attacker. There may have been other gates, but not enough remains to prove or disprove it.

Inside the citadel were houses. Much of this city still remains unexcavated because it would destroy other and more important levels to uncover all of it. However, it appears that there was a large house—a forerunner of the *megaron*, or great house—which was probably the ruler's palace. It was situated in the center of the city. The other houses were apparently separated and were not jammed together to use common walls as in so many old ruins. This indicates that only the nobility lived inside the walls.

Partly excavated wall of a Troy II *megaron* (great house) believed to be the palace of the king. The concave depression at left is part of a huge jar used for the storage of grain.

Not enough remains for us to tell whether the houses had windows. It is doubtful that they did. They appear to have had only a single door, and most contained only a single room. One of the better-preserved homes reveals an open hearth, lined with flat stones, in the center of the single room. Another house (but from the second period of the first Troy) had stone platforms along the wall, which could have been used for beds. Plaited matting remnants have been discovered, but no chairs or tables. Plates and tableware have not been discovered either. The first Trojans probably sat on the floor and ate from common cooking pots, using their hands for utensils.

They ate well, however. In one house excavators uncovered a clay-lined pit, which Blegen said was identical with kitchen receptacles later used by Turks to set bread to rise. This indicates, but does not prove, that the Trojans ate leavened bread, probably made from a sourdough base. Fortunately for archaeologists, the first Trojans were not a cleanly people. They dropped their bones and table refuse on the floor. When it became obnoxious, they covered it with a fresh layer of clay and started again. Bones found embedded in these clay garbage cans show that the Trojans ate beef, mutton, and pork regularly. Bones of rabbit and deer have also been found, but not as frequently as those of domesticated animals. Spits show that the meat was roasted over the open hearths.

Excavators also found loom weights and spindle whorls, which proved that they had learned to weave cloth, although they were definitely still in the period classified as the Late Aegean Stone Age. Utensils, weapons, and tools found in the debris of the first Troy were mainly stone. A rare piece of copper and a few pieces of bronze along with some lumps of lead show that they were familiar with metal, but had not begun to use it to a great extent.

However, Schliemann uncovered a mica slate mold that proved that the first Trojans probably used metal weapons to a greater extent than the ruins show. The mold was carved on all four sides with various shapes of arrowheads, spear points, and what may be knife blades. Later a number of other molds were found in Troy II, which indicated that a considerable armament industry went on within the city walls.

The stone weapons present a greater mystery than the metal ones. They indicate that Troy was not isolated, but had commerce with far places. Obsidian used for some of the weapons could only have come from the islands of the Aegean Sea. A number of very finely polished jade battle-axes were also found, and jade certainly did not come from any region near Troy. The discovery of a white jade battle-ax was expecially intriguing, for such stone is found only in China.

The first Troy lasted for five hundred years. Naturally there were changes in such a period of time, which is roughly equal in American history from the time of Columbus to 1960. Portions of the city were leveled and new houses built on top of their rubble. The characteristic pottery changed some, and the people moved deeper into the Early Aegean Bronze Age. They must have been comparatively peaceful years, for there is no indication of the fire and pillage that accompanied the sacking of ancient cities.

The end came, according to the Blegen chronology, about 2500 B.C. At about this same time Cheops was building the Great Pyramid of Egypt, the fascinating and mysterious Minoan civilization was just starting on the island of Crete, and the strange Indus River people were building the remarkable cities of Harappa and Mohenjo-Daro in present-day Pakistan.

At this time an earthquake completely leveled Troy. Cracks in the few remaining portions of the original wall prove the earthquake theory. There is no evidence of fire. Since these ancient cities, with so much wood and thatch construction, were especially vulnerable to fire, we can speculate that the destruction came late at night and in the summer time. Thus there were no cooking or heating fires to ignite the falling thatch roofs.

The number killed must have been tremendous, but there is no evidence of it. Schliemann found two male skeletons in the early levels, but because of his unscientific methods it is not always possible to tell in just exactly what level he made his discoveries. Some children's bones have been found formally buried within the city, but adult burials or cremations, as the case may prove to be, were done elsewhere. Although three successive groups of ar-chaeologists have hunted for them, no burial grounds from this period have been found. If people were killed in the earthquake, their bodies were removed before returning citizens leveled off the debris and began building the walls and houses of Troy II.

There was no break in culture. The builders of Troy II were the same people who lived in Troy I.

They leveled the rubble and in places smoothed the foundations with large pads of clay. The city walls were enlarged, and the new houses were better constructed. Troy II was a richer and more culturally advanced city, but still small. The fortified walls had a diameter of about 330 feet.

Troy II lasted three hundred years. The different levels of the city show that it was continually rebuilt. The fortifications were made stronger. Imposing towers were erected. A new type of corridor gate, more easy to defend, was cut in the walls.

The people of Troy II were as indifferent housekeepers as those who lived in Troy I. They also threw their bones and refuse on the floor and covered them with clay when they became obnoxious. This gives us a clear picture of what they had to eat. Pork, beef and sheep bones were as well represented as they were in Troy I, but there was an increase in fish and venison bones.

Although the city was well into the Early Aegean Bronze Age, excavators continued to find stone battle-axes. However, copper was extensively used and genuine bronze made its appearance in daggers, spearheads, and short swords. Gold was apparently plentiful. Schliemann's Great Treasure is attributed to this level. In addition, numerous golden beads, pins, and ornaments have been found in the debris of this city.

Destruction and rebuilding during the city's three hundred years produced seven distinct levels. Since the top stratum was characterized by extensive ashes and heat-seared rocks, Schliemann incorrectly labeled the underlying layers Troy II and called the top, or "burnt city," as he termed it, Troy III. He later corrected his mistake.

Little is known of Troy II's religion. Some raised portions of the houses may have served as a type of altar. Carl Schuchhardt (in

Schliemann's Excavations, 1891) reports on a curious lead idol found in the lower levels of Troy, but it cannot be identified with any particular level because of Schliemann's methods of digging. Schuchhardt says:

> It represents a nude female figure with long curls over her ears, and arms crossed on the breast. The strongly accentuated female characteristics mark it as the Asiatic Aphrodite. Similar figures of this deity in terra-cotta have been found in tombs of Mesopotamia and Cyprus, and stone ones in the Cyclades [Greek Aegean islands]. The swastika or hooked cross on the lower parts of the body so repeatedly found in all prehistoric sites . . . is Asiatic in origin. It seems to be the symbol of some ancient deity.

It is possible that the small lead idol (it is about two and a half inches tall) represents the Phrygian Mother of the Gods, Rhea. Phrygia, which borders the Troad, has been suggested as the home of the Trojans before they moved to Hissarlik. Strabo, the Greek geographer (63 to 24 B.C.?), writing almost two thousand years later, says, "The Phrygians generally, as well as those of the Trojans who live in the district of Ida, worship Rhea, and celebrate orgies in her honor, calling her the Mother of Gods."

The idol has definite Semitic characteristics, but on the other hand, the use of the swastika indicates an Aryan tie-in. However, the position of Troy, only a few miles from a natural crossroads between Europe and Asia (the Hellespont), would naturally bring the city into contact with many races. Schliemann believed that Phoenician traders came to Troy. In his book *Ilios*, Schliemann quotes an authority:

> Hissarlik lay in the track of the primitive migrations of the Indo-European race from their cradle in the East to their settlement in the West. This was not one migration only, but a passage to and fro between the shores of Asia and Europe. It was also the path of their commerce and military expeditions after they settled in their homes. . . . It must be borne in mind

The Dardanelles (the ancient Hellespont) is the strait between the Aegean Sea and the Sea of Marmara, which separates Asia and Europe. It is thirty-seven miles long, with an average width of three or four miles. It is one mile wide at its narrowest point. Troy lies beyond the faint hills showing in the distance.

that the Hellespont and the Bosporus (as the latter name [cattle crossing] expresses) were *ferries* rather than sundering seas.

The fact that Troy was located in such a stragetic communications position has led to considerable scholarly speculation about how the Trojans made their living. We know from physical evidence found in the ruins that they were herdsmen of large flocks and herds. Beans, peas, and wheat found in the ruins show that they cultivated extensive fields. In fact, Homer says that one wheat field extended to the walls of Troy.

However, an economy based upon agriculture and husbandry would hardly account for the rich personal ornaments that Schliemann found in the levels of Troy II. Where did the gold come from? It has been suggested that the Trojan king levied a toll on travelers and merchants passing through his land. Another theory is that the Trojans were pirates, preying on the ships that passed through the Hellespont. There is nothing to support either view, other than Troy's location. Piracy, of course, is in keeping with the spirit of the times. The entire Aegean Sea was a nest of pirates. Even trading ships were piratical to a degree. In the *Histories* of Herodotus we read how the Phoenician traders spent six days selling their wares in Argos, Greece. Then, finishing their business, they stole women and whatever else was available and sailed away.

The rise of Troy II in importance and the development of the still strange Minoan empire on the island of Crete occurred at about the same time. Despite much excavation on Crete, the early history of the island is not clear. A legendary king named Minos built the foundations of the empire by constructing a powerful fleet that suppressed piracy in the Aegean area.

There is no evidence as to when Minos lived. Some think that Minos was the title of a ruler rather than the name of an individual man, as "pharaoh" was the title of Egyptian kings. In any event, Crete is a small island about 320 miles south of Troy. A narrow island 160 miles long could hardly have supported the astonishingly rich Minoan civilization without strong trade, and this trade could not have flourished without Minoan control of the seas. All this supports the legends of Minos' great navy and his battles with the Aegean pirates.

So much is sound history. What comes next is supposition, but the guesses are based upon such meager archaeological information as is available. Troy II was destroyed by fire—a fire so great that the flames actually melted the crusts of some sun-dried bricks, vitrifying them—turning them into glass.

What brought about such devastating destruction? The fire was not caused by an earthquake, for there are no cracked stones and walls as Schliemann found in Troy I. Could the fire have been caused by an accident? Can we postulate a Trojan cow to place in history beside the famous Trojan Horse? Could she have kicked over a torch, as Mrs. O'Leary's cow reputedly did to start Chicago's great fire? An accident is possible, but the fury of the fire—judging by its effects—indicates deliberate arson.

Most investigators lean to the theory that Troy II was destroyed in war. But whom were the Trojans fighting? The war was certainly not widespread. The ruins of contemporary Kum Tepe, on the coast three miles from Troy, do not show similar destruction. There is not even a local legend or tradition to explain what must have been an important event.

The Hittites of central Anatolia had not yet become powerful enough to launch a war. There is no evidence that the early Greeks could have done so either. If Mesopotamia or Egypt sacked Troy, there should have been records of it in those countries. Crete then appears to have been the only power capable of destroying such a powerfully walled city.

We can speculate then that Minos of Crete grew tired of Trojan piracy against Minoan ships in the Hellespont and sacked the city as part of his war to pacify the Aegean Sea.

Set against this argument is evidence that there was no prolonged siege. The Trojans appear to have quit the doomed city in a panic. Blegen says, "It is obvious that the catastrophe struck suddenly, without warning, giving the inhabitants little or no time to collect and save their most treasured belongings." He goes on to say that practically every building in the city showed abandoned bits of gold and jewelry. In one place there were the charred remnants of a great loom. Near it were found 189 gold beads of fifteen different shapes. We can speculate that the beads were to be woven into a royal garment. Blegen believed that they might have been part of a necklace whose string has long since rotted away.

On the other hand, the treasures found by Schliemann indicate that there may have been ample warning. In one case Schliemann found gold hairpins, earrings, beads, and necklaces stuffed in a broken pottery jar. Of the Great Treasure (which he called the Treasure of King Priam), Schliemann said, "I found all of these articles together, forming a quadrangular mass. It seems certain that they were placed on the city-wall in a wooden chest, such as those mentioned by Homer as being in the Palace of King Priam."

Here Schliemann is referring to the scene in the *Iliad* where Priam goes to his treasure chest to take out gold to ransom the dead body of his son Hector from Achilles.

> It is possible [Schliemann continued] that in the conflagration some one hurriedly packed the treasure in a chest. . . . When he reached the wall, however, the hand of the enemy or the fire overtook him. He was obliged to abandon the chest, which was immediately covered to a height of 5 to 6 feet with the reddish or yellow ashes and the bricks of the adjoining royal houses.

Schliemann goes on to say that later he found other smaller treasures near the same location. This led him to an alternate theory that all the treasures fell to the place where he found them when a towerlike building burned and collapsed.

The stratum comprising the burned city averages about nine feet in depth. The heavy ashes indicate that there was considerable timber used in construction. A lot of the so-called ashes, however, proved to be decomposed brick. Although fired brick was not used in construction, the tremendous heat of the fire affected large portions of the originally unbaked clay.

Schliemann was always eager to share his discoveries with colleagues. In 1879 he invited Professor Emile Burnouf of Paris to inspect the ruins. After studying what Schliemann had uncovered, Burnouf decided that the fire was driven by a strong wind from the southwest toward the northeast. The ashes and debris were especially heavy in the center of the town, where Schliemann believed the ruler's palace had stood. Here the debris was thirteen feet deep. Burnouf said, "The house from which they are derived must have been two, perhaps three, storeys high."

Schliemann wrote, "For a very long distance on the north side there was, at a depth of from 26 to 30 feet, a sort of vitrified [glassy] sheet, which was only interrupted by house walls."

The ceilings of the building were made of crossed timbers covered with clay to make a smooth surface. Schliemann says, "This clay seems to have been more or less fused by the burning of the beams. In fact, only in this manner can we explain the enormous mass of vitrified lumps in the ruins. These were either shapeless or of a conical form, and often from 5 to 6 inches thick."

The clay had been mixed with straw as reinforcement when it was put on the roofs. Dr. Edward Moss, a surgeon from a British ship that stopped at Besika Bay below Troy, told Schliemann that silica in the straw probably helped the intense heat turn the clay into an alumina glass, which accounted for the vitrified lumps.

For lack of better evidence, we can ascribe the destruction of Troy II to invaders, arson by revolutionists, arson by a disgruntled person or persons, or an accident.

Strangely enough, the known facts do not accord with any of these. If there were invaders strong enough to breach the admittedly strong fortifications of Troy II, why was so much gold left in the ruins? Why were there no skeletons or at least the charred bones of defenders who fell in the battle? If the fire was the result of accident or malicious design, we would still expect to find the bones of people who must have been burned or asphyxiated by the smoke.

The logical answer of the mystery of the missing dead is that the people of Troy returned after the disaster and buried their dead. No cemetery of this period has yet been discovered. There are indications that the people were cremated and perhaps buried in jars. On the other hand, the remains of some babies and children were buried under homes, presumably—archaeologists tell us—because the children were in need of protection. But if this was the reason, why weren't there more of them? Child mortality must have been high in those days.

However, if the bodies of those killed in the destruction of Troy II were removed and buried or burned, why did the burial crews neglect to collect the gold and treasure scattered about the city? Archaeologists are ready to make assumptions on scarce evidence, but they exclaim in horror if one mentions ancient curses. Be that as it may, a belief in a curse or the dissatisfaction of some strange god could account for the lack of bodies and the untouched treasure.

The ground itself was certainly not accursed. People of the same culture as Troy II built Troy III on the same spot, leveling the ruins to provide a foundation for the new city. In doing so they certainly should have found Priam's Treasure and the other caches of valuables that Schliemann uncovered if indeed these fell from an upper story of the burning palace.

This brings up another point. Was Troy as rich as it has been reputed to be? Schliemann said the treasures came from the stratum of the "burnt city." Later investigators have not challenged him. However, Schliemann was admittedly not a scientific investigator during these early excavations. He dug frantically, without regard to stratification. He was after treasure. He believed he would find it in the layer just above bedrock, for he then thought that Homer's Troy would be the first city on the Hissarlik outcropping.

Stratification is the name for debris left in individual layers by a succession of geological or human actions. Today archaeologists uncover these strata one by one, like peeling back the layers of an onion. Each stratum is delicately treated. Sometimes excavators use dental picks and camel's-hair brushes to remove particles with extreme care. Each layer is exhaustively photographed and marked into grids, and all pertinent information is recorded. The records will note the color of the soil, its texture, composition, depth, and all foreign matter trapped in it. They will also include the position of such matter.

This care is necessary to define a stratum clearly, but a stratum, unfortunately, is not a clearly defined layer. Stratification is complicated by distortions, interruptions, and disturbances.

Distortions can be caused by uneven levels that have been filled in at later times. Disturbances may be caused by water seepages, cracking of the ground, and displacements due to earthquakes. An arrowhead, for example, dislodged from a higher stratum could fall through an earthquake crack and end up in a layer put there a thousand years before its time.

Interruptions are artificial disruptions of strata. The foundations of new buildings may be dug deep into older layers. Post molds—an archaeological term for areas where posts were sunk into the ground—are also interruptions that must be skillfully determined and plotted to avoid dislocating time.

Considering the way Schliemann made these initial excavations, there is a possibility that the treasures he uncovered in the layers of Troy II could have been buried in holes dug in a later period—possibly in Troy VI, the greatest of the archaeological Troys. This is speculative and is mentioned here solely to point out the absolute need to make complete documentation when digging in an archaeological site. Otherwise, there is always the possibility that doubt will taint the discoveries.

The diadem found in Priam's Treasure was of exceptional work, better than one would assume for the time. According to Schliemann, there were 16,353 separate pieces in the large diadem. He reports that a London goldsmith inspected the diadem and said, "All the idols and leaves of both diadems were cut out with a bronze punch from thin gold plate. To make the very thin wire the Trojans could have used only ingots of very pure gold, which they forced through the holes of a draw-plate. Alloyed gold could not have been used to make such fine wire." This again raises some doubt about the correctness of definitely assigning the find to Troy II.

On the other hand, if the treasure did in fact originate in Troy II, the failure of the builders of Troy III to find it can be explained by the passing of a long period between the fall of the city and the rise of the new capital. The walls of houses in these early cities were built of sun-dried bricks placed upon stone foundations. In time the torrential rains reduced the bricks back to layers of clay. Such clay could well have covered the treasures.

There is no way of determining how much time elapsed between the fall of Troy II and the rise of Troy III. The basic culture did not change, indicating that the same type of people rebuilt the place. That does not necessarily indicate they were exactly the same people who fled the burning city. The rebuilding might have taken place five, ten, twenty, fifty, or even a hundred years after the fire. Culture developed slowly in 2200 B.C., the approximate time of Troy II's destruction.

3

THE LATER TROYS

The rage of the Turkish government at being cheated of its share of Priam's Treasure prevented Schliemann from returning immediately to Hissarlik. He was not greatly concerned. He felt that he had accomplished his twin objectives. He had found Homer's Troy and Priam's Treasure. Later, when he began to doubt his identification of Troy II as Homer's Troy, he put in applications for a new firman. In the meantime, however, he turned his attention to Mycenae, which Homer had identified as the home of Agamemnon, leader of the Argives who fought in the Trojan War.

Here he had a different objective. At Hissarlik he had been trying to prove that there really had been a historical Troy. Mycenae did not have to be proved. It was there below Corinth in the form of cyclopean walls atop a high hill on the Plain of Argos on Greece's Peloponnesian Peninsula. Mycenae had never been lost, and travelers throughout history had visited the ruins to marvel at the famous Lion Gate, which opened into the huge stone walls.

Schliemann and Sophia began digging at Mycenae in February 1874, seven months after smuggling the Great Treasure out of Turkey. In hunting for the remains of Agamemnon, Schliemann put his trust in Pausanias, the first-century Greek traveler and writer.

Mycenae, once the capital of a great empire in the Heroic Age, had been destroyed in 468 B.C., and when Pausanias visited the place, it had already been in ruins for more than five hundred years, and Agamemnon had been dead for about 1,300 years.

Pausanias wrote:

> Some remains of the circuit wall [of Mycenae] are still to be seen, and the gate which has the lions over it. These were built, they say, by the Cyclopes, who made the wall at Tiryns. . . . There is a tomb of Atreus [father of Agamemnon] and his children where their treasures are kept. There is the tomb of those whom Aigisthos [Aegisthus] slew at the banquet, on their return from Ilium with Agamemnon. Cassandra's tomb is there, but its authenticity is denied by the Lacedaemonians of Amykalae. [Cassandra was the prophetess daughter of Priam of Troy.] There is also the tomb of Agamemnon. . . . Clytemnestra and Aigisthos were buried a little way outside the wall, for they were not thought worthy to be within, where Agamemnon lay and those who fell with him.

Clytemnestra was the faithless wife of Agamemnon who arranged for her lover, Aegisthus, to murder Agamemnon upon his return from the sack of Troy. Aeschylus, Sophocles, and Euripides all developed powerful plays from this ancient triangle. Clytemnestra was the sister of Helen of Troy.

The statement of Pausanias that Clytemnestra and Aegisthus were buried outside the wall convinced Schliemann that Agamemnon's tomb would be found inside the citadel walls. Others had assumed that the Greek writer meant the outer city walls. After clearing debris from in front of the Lion Gate, Schliemann decided to excavate within a curious circle of stones just inside the gate. Here in 1876, with luck as unbelievable as his great fortune in finding the Trojan treasure, Schliemann uncovered five graves, including treasure that surpassed that of Troy.

The most dramatic of the treasures were three splendid gold masks. One, larger than the rest, showed a majestic face. It caused Schliemann to cry, "I have gazed on the face of Agamemnon!"

"I have gazed on the face of Agamemnon," Schliemann said when he found this golden mask at Mycenae. Today's archaeologists believe it came from an earlier age. Woodcut from Schliemann's *Mycenae*.

But again Schliemann, for all his luck, was wrong. Just as he had mistaken the Troy II stratum for Homer's Ilium, he was also mistaken about the golden mask being a portrait of Agamemnon. The history of Mycenae is as mysterious as that of Troy, and there has been no satisfactory identification of the mask, but archaeologists now believe that it shows the face of a king who preceded Agamemnon by at least two hundred years.

All Schliemann got from his Mycenae discoveries was glory. The Greek government had strict laws forbidding the export of antiquities, and government officials closely watched everything Schliemann did.

The Mycenae treasures created a sensation when exhibited later in the year in Athens, but in the midst of his triumph Schliemann was dissatisfied. The arguments put forth by those who challenged his claim of discovering Troy continued to rankle. Some of them were strong arguments, and Schliemann himself was hard put to defend his claims. He was now anxious to get back to Troy and uncover more positive evidence.

Several things worked in his favor. The Turkish government had been pleased at Schliemann's grand gesture in presenting them with five times the original court award. He had stipulated that the money must be used to build up the National Museum in Istanbul. Also the publicity and honor that he received as a result of the Mycenae finds had made him the world's best-known archaeologist after Sir Austen Layard. Layard happened to be British ambassador to Turkey, and he put strong pressure upon the Turks to renew Schliemann's firman. This was done under surprisingly favorable terms.

The firman was to begin in September, 1878. With a few hot summer months to kill before he could begin a new dig at Troy, Schliemann and Sophia went to the island of Ithaca, seeking the palace of Odysseus. He uncovered some ruins, but the result, in the main, was disappointing, and he returned to Troy for the fourth time.

His amazing luck still held. He discovered two small treasure troves on October 21, 1878, after less than two months of digging. He was allowed to retain only one third of what he found. Under the terms of his firman two thirds of all discoveries must be handed over to the National Museum. Officials were appointed to watch his every move and to see that he kept to his agreement.

Schliemann went to Hissarlik again in 1879 and worked over the old ground. He uncovered more of Troy II, which he still insisted was Homer's Troy. His health was deteriorating badly. Also, his temper was growing shorter, and he constantly raged against those who refused to believe him. He had taken young Wilhelm Dörpfeld as an assistant. Dörpfeld, influenced by the work of Flinders Petrie and E. A. Wallis Budge in Egypt, insisted upon a more scientific approach to the Trojan excavations. He cataloged and kept records where the impatient Schliemann had brushed aside all that did not interest him.

Dörpfeld never publicly criticized Schliemann, but the crotchety old man must have been a trial to the younger archaeologist. Once while on a trip to Egypt between digging seasons, he wrote an apologetic letter to Dörpfeld. He was dying and seemed to know it, but he still tried to pack in as much work as possible in those last years.

Earlier (in 1880) Schliemann had disposed of the Great Treasure. Some of the greatest museums of the world had offered to buy it, but money meant nothing to him anymore. He claimed in 1890 that one half of his annual income went for living expenses for himself and his family, and for his excavations. This left a full half to add to his capital. By this time he and Sophia had two children, a daughter he had named Andromaché, after Hector's faithful wife, and a son named Telemachus, for the son of Odysseus.

After much soul-searching, he finally made a decision. He loved Greece, but he said that only two countries had treated him kindly, the United States and Germany. He wavered between the two, but in the end his German blood made the decision. The treasure was given to a museum in Berlin that would bear his name. In return the German government paid him high honors, including a personally written letter of commendation from Kaiser Wilhelm I.

Sophia Schliemann was infuriated. She wanted the treasure to go to her native Greece. She had a way of bending the grumpy old man to her will, but this time she had failed. Although he had lived in many countries and still held American citizenship, which he never renounced, at the end Schliemann was a German.

He continued to dig in Troy, but made no other big finds. He worked in Tiryns, another great Mycenaean center, and tried to buy land to dig in Crete. It had become clear that the roots of Mycenae lay in Crete. In some manner the Minoans, who may have been the invaders who destroyed Troy II, fathered the succeeding Mycenaean empire that later, under Agamemnon, destroyed the real Homeric Troy.

Schliemann, to Dörpfeld's anguish, was unable to buy the land. The deal was almost made at one time, but Schliemann broke off negotiations in a temper because he thought owners of the land were trying to outsmart him. Later, Sir Arthur Evans of England excavated in the area that Schliemann had selected and uncovered the magnificent ruins of Knossos. Thus Schliemann was denied his last great triumph.

In 1889, infuriated because a scientific gathering in Paris had ridiculed his claims, Schliemann invited a group to Hissarlik to view his work. Then in 1890 he invited ten of the most distinguished men he could get to come again. They included internationally known men from France, Turkey, Germany, and England.

In a letter signed by all ten, they did not claim the ruins to be Troy, but they did demolish the claim that Hissarlik was a necropolis and verified that the ruins were an important Early Bronze Age city. They also certified that the floor plan of the ruins of the second city resembled those of Mycenae.

This claim brushed aside world doubt. If there ever had been a real Troy, this must be it.

Unfortunately, Schliemann had only one year left to enjoy his triumph. He died while on a trip to Italy, and his body was brought back and buried according to his desires in Athens. His work in Troy was carried on by Dörpfeld. In time Dörpfeld changed his views about Troy II and decided that the Homeric Troy was really Troy VI, the most splendid of all the nine Troys. The intervening Troy III, IV, and V he dismissed as "miserable villages."

Carl W. Blegen, leader of the Cincinnati Expedition to Troy, excavated some undisturbed layers and disagreed. He found that Troys III, IV, and V were more important than Dörpfeld had assumed. They were settled by the same type of people who built Troy I and II, but they were obviously not as rich as the Trojans of the burned city. Their homes were jammed closer together. Most independent houses had disappeared in favor of apartment-type dwellings with common walls. One major difference was that the walls in Troy III were all stone, whereas those of Troy II were sun-dried brick built upon a raised stone foundation. Blegen surmised that stone was used because the ruins of Troy II left so many rocks that building with stone was easier than making bricks.

The pottery used in Troy III did not change much from that used in the previous city. A curious pot made with human faces molded on it was used in both cities, but those of Troy III showed improved skill.

Troy III lasted 150 years, from about 2200 B.C. to 2050 B.C. in Blegen's chronology. Ilhan Aksit of the Canakkale Museum dates the third Troy from 2300 to 2200, which is a hundred years earlier than Blegen, and limits its time to only one century.

Troy III ended, was leveled, and became the foundation for Troy IV. There is no evidence as to the cause of its destruction. There were no cracked walls to indicate an earthquake, no evidence of an unusual fire, and nothing to indicate vandalism by invaders. It has been suggested that the people were carried off by a plague and that after a suitable time others of their race leveled the deserted buildings and built a new city. There is nothing to support or refute such a theory. The Third Trojans came, built a city, lived in it from 100 to 150 years, and left only a six-foot layer of rubble to show that they had ever lived at all.

The walls of Troy III cannot be determined, but apparently they enclosed a larger area than Troy II, although they were probably not as imposing. Troy IV was definitely a larger city in size than any previous Troy. Like Troy III, not much is known about it because so much of its stratum was destroyed by Schliemann in his anxiety to expose Troy II. The pottery shows that Troy IV was a continuation of the previous culture, although the potter's wheel had come into more general use. Troy IV lasted 150 years in Blegen's chronology and 100 years in Aksit's. Blegen dates it from 2050 to 1900, and Aksit from 2200 to 2100 B.C. Like Troy III, it came to an end without leaving us a clue to the reason why.

Troy V was better built than any of the previous cities, although

In this section of Schliemann's great ditch, remnants of Troy II and III show in the lower sections, and the ruins of Troy VI tower above them at left.

a shortage of rock caused them to use more sun-dried brick. The houses were neater, because the Fifth Trojans had started to clean their homes instead of throwing refuse on the floor and covering it with clay. This did not endear the inhabitants to the excavators. Blegen said that archaeologists could hardly be blamed for feeling a prejudice against these Trojans. They had robbed excavators of many of the telltale articles that reveal how people lived and what they ate.

The new homes exhibited benches and seats made of clay and a widespread use of a beehive oven first introduced in Troy IV. These ovens also had flues, the first indication of how smoke was carried out of the houses. It was assumed that in the earlier homes smoke rose through a hole in the roof in the manner of many American Indian dwellings.

Very few artifacts were found. The ones excavators did find showed that bronze was now widely used. According to Blegen the first levels of Troy V showed pottery comparable to that of Troy IV, but in the late phases it had improved both in technical skill and in artistic quality.

A newborn baby's bones were found buried under one floor. In another location excavators found a man's leg bone. No other burials were found in or outside the city.

Blegen's opinion was "that had the life of this town been extended by a half-century or a century, the Fifth Settlement would probably have evolved and created a notable and highly distinctive era of Early Bronze Age culture."

Troy V lasted from 1900 to 1800 B.C. in the Blegen chronology and from 2100 to 1900 according to Aksit. As with the two preceding Troys, there is no clue to why or how the city fell. The ending of Troy V is more mysterious and intriguing than that of any of the previous cities, for it rang down the curtain on the early Trojan race. Studies of pottery and other cultural artifacts indicate clearly that each time Troy was destroyed, men of the same culture rebuilt on the ruins of old cities, but with the fall of Troy V, these people vanished completely from the archaeological scene.

The first people came to Hissarlik in 3000 B.C., and their

descendants occupied the growing mound in five distinct cities and through 1200 years. They survived earthquakes, fires, and unknown causes of total destruction, and then vanished completely, leaving no record of where they came from, where they went, or what they looked like.

Various theories have been advanced about the origin of the first Trojans. They may have come out of the Caucasus region and migrated down through Turkey to the Troad. Some experts think they may have come out of Thrace to cross the Bosporus, or Hellespont, into Asia. Others have wondered if they wandered up from Mesopotamia. Still another possibility is that they came in boats from the Aegean Sea islands and landed first at Kum Tepe on the coast before moving inland to the better-protected Hissarlik.

These various theories are based upon isolated finds in the several levels of Troy. The finding of the Asiatic mother-goddess statue indicates to some theorists (guessers, actually) the Asiatic origin of the first Trojans. Other artifacts clearly indicate their Cyclades Islands origin. Some indicate contact with the Phoenicians. However, the position of Troy at the crossroads of Europe and Asia, both as to land and sea routes, must naturally have brought them into contact with many different peoples. This alone can account for the various objects of strange cultures. Basically, however, the remains of the first five Troys show a steady development of a single culture that cannot be definitely tied to any other known one of their times.

The next city, Troy VI, was in existence from 1800 to 1300 B.C. (Blegen), or from 1900 to 1300 (Aksit). The two disagree on the date of the founding, but agree on the date of its destruction. The indications are strong that a completely different people built the Sixth Troy. The new people were Homer's Trojans and are believed to have been of the same stock as the Mycenaean Greeks.

It is not strange for one race to have supplanted another in these barbaric times, but it is strange indeed that the new Trojans did not retain any of the traditions of those who came before them.

The Greek tradition of Troy is, of course, based upon Homer's

Part of the city walls not destroyed by the great earthquake that leveled Troy VI.

Iliad and *Odyssey*. These epics tell of the destruction of Troy VII-a and what came after it. There are references in the *Odyssey* and in other Greek accounts to the destruction of the city prior to the Trojan War. This accords with archaeological evidence of the destruction of Troy VI by a devastating earthquake. Beyond this the Greeks are silent about the mysterious men who lived for 1200 years on the spot where sacred Ilium was built.

This may indicate that quite a number of years passed between the fall of Troy V and the building of Troy VI. Neither the first Trojans nor their contemporaries in history left any writing to supplement the little that archaeology can tell us of the first inhabitants of Hissarlik.

4

THE TIME OF LEGENDS

Carl Blegen, of the Cincinnati Expedition, dug in the ruins for seven seasons, beginning in 1932. The ruins had been undisturbed since the end of Dörpfeld's excavations in 1894. Blegen had the advantage of more refined archaeological methods. He was thus able to correct many of the errors of both Schliemann and Dörpfeld. He invited Dörpfeld, then in his eighties, to visit Troy again, and Dörpfeld, after some hesitation, agreed with the American's interpretations.

It was Blegen who determined the culture break between Troy V and Troy VI. "The changes seem to me to be so unheralded [Blegen wrote], so widespread, and so far-reaching that they can only be explained as indicating a break with the past, and the arrival and establishment on the site of a new people with a heritage of its own."

Blegen believed that the settlers of Troy VI were early Greeks. He based his opinion upon the wide use of gray Minyan ware, a distinctive pottery made both in Troy VI and on the Greek mainland. He conjectured that the basic migration split into two sections, one going into Greece through Thrace and the other into Asia Minor.

"Regarding their origin and the earlier home from which they set out, no convincing theory has yet been put forward," he said.

The Troy VI Trojans were the first to introduce the horse into the Troad. Homer comments upon the Trojans' skill with horses. This seems to rule out assumptions that these people came by boat through the Black Sea, for it would have been more difficult to ship the animals in the frail craft of the time than it would have been to ride them.

Whoever the men were who built Troy VI, they already knew how to build a city. They certainly were not nomads or barbarians. They were city dwellers who were used to the best of their time, which was the Middle Aegean Bronze Age. The imposing walls they built for Troy VI showed that they understood military engineering. Inside the walls were free-standing houses built upon terraces, something new for Troy.

Little was done to explore these upper stratifications during the lifetime of Schliemann, for he was only interested in Troy II. But after his death Dörpfeld concentrated more on these other levels. In 1894 he found in the sixth level considerable Mycenaean pottery, which had obviously been imported. This pottery was a tremendous help in dating the Sixth Troy.

It is, as mentioned earlier, extremely difficult to date archaeological finds precisely. However, if an excavator can find in his digs objects that can tie his ruins with other known periods, then he can more accurately pinpoint dates for his excavations.

The Mycenaean pottery definitely established Troy VI as being contemporary with the period of Mycenae's greatest power. Since the Mycenaeans under Agamemnon were the ones who fought the Trojan War, the presence of the pottery convinced Dörpfeld that Schliemann had been wrong and that Troy VI, not Troy II, had been destroyed by the vengeful Greek.

Dörpfeld's theory was accepted by both the scientific and literary world for forty years, until 1936, when Blegen's work with the Cincinnati Expedition convinced Dörpfeld that he had been wrong also, and that Troy VII-a was the Homeric city. However, Dörpfeld's work on Troy VI was extremely important, for this city was the greatest of all the nine Troys.

About half of the original wall of Troy VI still remains or can be traced. This is partly because a lot of Troy VII-a's walls made use of portions of the sixth city's fortifications. Presumably the king's megaron was on a hill in the center of the expanded city wall, but nothing was ever found of it because the hill was cleared and flattened in Roman times to build a courtyard for the temple of Athena. Schliemann has often been condemned for destroying the temple to get to Troy II.

Both Blegen and Dörpfeld uncovered the remains of tremendous towers around the gates of Troy VI. The towers had a batter so that they sloped inward toward the top. This provided wide bases for greater stability. The large limestone blocks at the bottom were polished to make it harder for attackers to scale the wall. On top there probably were ramparts so that defenders could hurl stones and missiles down upon the attackers. After inspecting the ruins of the southwest gate, which Dörpfeld had originally uncovered, Blegen called it "a masterpiece of military engineering."

A small cemetery was discovered outside the walls in 1934, the first mass burial place to be found in all the Troys. The bodies had been burned and the ashes placed in clay jars for burial.

Both Blegen and Aksit agree that Troy VI was destroyed in 1300 B.C. One of the major contributions of the Cincinnati Expedition of 1932–1938 was the discovery that Troy VI was destroyed by an earthquake of great intensity. Dörpfeld rejected this theory at first. In 1936 he wrote an article in German defending his belief that Troy VI was the true Ilium. However, after visiting the ruins for the first time since his last work in the 1890's, he agreed with Blegen that Troy VII-a was the Homeric city. Blegen showed him great masses of wall stones that the Cincinnati Expedition had uncovered. They had unmistakably resulted when great sections of the wall collapsed under terrific pressure. Blegen said such destruction was beyond anything human hands could have done before the invention of explosives. The venerable Dörpfeld agreed.

Both history, as revealed by archaeology, and legend agree with this theory of Troy VI's end. Historically, according to Aksit, an earthquake did occur about the time estimated for the city's destruction. It was so great that it was felt over a wide area of Asia Minor.

At this point, to lead into the mythological account of the "earth-shaking" that collapsed Troy's walls, we must mix the various accounts of Herodotus, Strabo, Apollodorus, and mythology. At the time the supposedly Greek people founded Troy, this section of Asia Minor was populated by three major divisions of people. In the vicinity of Troy were the Teucrians. To the northeast of these were

The portion of wall in the foreground contains burned stones from Troy VI. Higher up the hill is a portion of an outcropping of stones from Troy VIII.

the Phrygians. Far to the south were the remnants of the Carians, who had been the dominant people until their power was broken by the rise of the Minos kings of Crete.

Strabo claims that the Phrygians came from Thrace across the Bosporus. Another account claims that the Phrygians fathered the Teucrians, or that the Teucrians also came from Thrace. Strabo, however, draws on old traditions that claim the Teucrians came from Crete. This is important because Herodotus states positively that it was the Teucrians who built Troy VI. If he is correct, it does not negate the theory that the Trojans who supplanted the original people of Troy were early Greeks.

Mycenae, the first great development in ancient Greece, was settled by a Stone Age people who migrated from the north. In time Mycenae came under the influence of the seagoing Cretans. Artifacts and beautiful frescoes showing acrobats leaping over the horns of bulls, uncovered by Schliemann in Mycenaean ruins, are identical with those found by Sir Arthur Evans in Crete. This leaves no doubt that the Cretans were Mycenae's cultural teachers. In time Mycenae grew in power, whereas Crete declined. In the years coinciding with the foundation of Troy VI, Mycenae occupied Knossos, the capital of Crete. Therefore, we do not distort any known historical fact if we believe that Mycenaean Greeks from Crete did indeed migrate to the Troad.

Schliemann summarized Strabo's account in this manner:

> An oracle had bidden the Teucrians to settle down in the place where they should be assailed by earth creatures. This happened when an immense host of field mice came forth from the ground, and gnawed away all the leather of their arms and utensils. There consequently they established themselves and called the mountain Ida after the mountain of that name in Crete.

Now in a tradition preserved by Apollodorus (in *The Library*, a compilation of Greek mythology), two brothers lived on the island of Samothrace, whose peaks to the northwest of the Troad are visible from Troy on a clear day. One brother was killed by a heavenly thunderbolt, and the other, Dardanus, fled from Samothrace. He went to the land of the Teucrians, who took their name from their leader Teucer. Dardanus, being from Samothrace, was of Thracian origin. Teucer is identified as being the son of the River Scamander (which flowed past Troy) and a nymph from Mount Ida. If there is any historical basis for this legend, the Bunarbashi ruins should be the home of the Teucrians.

Dardanus married Teucer's daughter and became king when his father-in-law died. He renamed the country Dardania. We now go to Homer for the continuation of the story: "Then Dardanus begat a son, King Erichthonios, who became the richest of mortal men. . . . Then Erichthonios begat Tros to be lord over the Trojans, and to Tros three noble sons were born, Ilos, Assarakos and godlike Ganymede."

Ganymede was so beautiful that Zeus, king of the gods, took the youth to Olympus to be his cupbearer. According to both Apollodorus and Hellanicus, Zeus gave Tros a team of immortal horses in payment for Ganymede.

Assarakos remained in the ancestral home on the slopes of Mount Ida and became the great-great-grandfather of Aeneas, the hero of Vergil's epic *The Aeniad*. Ilos went to Phrygia, where he won the wrestling crown in the annual games. His reward was fifty youths and fifty maidens, plus a cow of many colors. According to a Phrygian oracle, he was to build a city for his fifty couples where the cow should lie down.

Ilos faithfully followed the cow, who wandered a long way before she finally rested on the mound at Hissarlik.

There was a small shrine to the Phrygian Até on the mound. This is the only reference in Greek accounts of any structures at Hissarlik before Ilos built Troy VI and called it Ilium after his own name.

The presence of the Phrygian temple on the mound does not indicate that the previous inhabitants of Troy V were Phrygians. It does indicate that considerable time passed between the fall of Troy

V and the building of Troy VI. During those years the heavy rains of the Troad winter had melted the sun-dried brick so that the clay flowed around the stones. Grass, weeds, and flowers grew in the soil, and the first five Troys were buried, not to be exposed until Schliemann came along more than 3,600 years later. Not even a hint of the first five Troys can be found in the Greek legends.

The Phrygian goddess Até was Zeus's oldest daughter. She irritated her father so badly that he cast her out of Olympus. In time Até grew into the Trojan Athena. According to Schliemann, "The Ilian Athené, who originated from this Até, appears on a medal wearing a Phrygian cap."

Schliemann put great faith in this legend. In his book, *Ilios*, he wrote, "The legend of the foundation of Ilium is by no means a frivolous or childish invention of Apollodorus, but an ancient legend of primitive growth, which is devised with beautiful symbolism." However, he did not believe that the fifty boys and girls actually came with Ilos from Phrygia to found Troy. Schliemann thought them symbolic of the fifty weeks of the year.

Upon the death of Ilos, rule of his city on Hissarlik mound passed to his son Laomedon, along with the immortal horses that Zeus had given Tros. Laomedon had five sons, the youngest of whom was named Podarces.

Apparently Laomedon got on well with Zeus, at least in the beginning. When Laomedon needed stronger walls for Troy, Zeus detailed Apollo and Poseidon to build them. Homer does not include this account, but makes a reference to it in Book XX of the *Iliad*, which shows that he was familiar with the tradition.

What happened next was reported in *Hellanicus*, a fifth-century-B.C. chronicle:

Poseidon and Apollo, having been commanded by Zeus to serve Laomedon king of Troy for hire, builded him a wall for a certain reward, but Laomedon broke his oaths and the covenant, and drove them away without their wage. Whereupon Poseidon, being wroth, sent a sea-beast against the land, and the people perished, and the fruits.

So Laomedon sought to the oracle, that bade him sacrifice his daughter, Hesione, to the monster. Whereupon Laomedon exposed her, but offered a reward, namely the immortal horses of Zeus, to him that would slay the thing and save Hesione.

The great hero Heracles (Hercules) heard of the offer and came to Troy, but even his tremendous strength did not appear to be enough to vanquish so terrible a monster. He called on Athena for help, and the goddess built him a protective wall on the beach below Troy. He hid behind it until the monster came out of the sea.

"Then Heracles leaped down the mouth and into the belly of the sea-beast, and tore its flank and it died."

Laomedon, as perfidious as when he robbed Poseidon and Apollo of their wages, now cheated Heracles by giving him two ordinary horses instead of the promised immortal steeds of Zeus.

The great hero was in a rage. He went to Poseidon for help, and the sea god, while annoyed at the way Heracles had killed the sea beast he had sent against Troy, agreed to help. Poseidon, in addition to ruling the oceans, was also known as the Earth Shaker. He shook the Troad until the great walls he and Apollo had built collapsed. Heracles and his followers then defeated the Trojans and killed Laomedon.

The king's five sons were captured, but Heracles agreed to permit one to live so that Troy would not be without a king. Heracles himself was a wanderer and did not want the Trojan crown for himself. He permitted Hesione, the girl he had saved from the sea beast, to choose which son would live. She picked Podarces, the youngest.

Heracles then told the girl that Podarces was his slave by right of conquest and that he could not part with him without a price, but she could name whatever price she wished to pay for her brother. She paid for him with her veil, which Heracles gallantly accepted. And thereafter Podarces was known as Priam, which means "ransomed." Under his leadership the Trojans repaired their shattered walls and established a new city about which Homer would later sing his inspired epics.

If we strip away the mythological gods and heroes, this story accords exactly with archaeological evidence uncovered at Troy. It explains the ruins at Bunarbashi, the settlement of the area by people of Thracean descent, the building of Troy on Hissarlik, and its destruction by a great earthquake. The rebuilding of the city by the same people who lived there before the great earthquake also is in accord with the archaeological evidence. And finally, this rebuilt city was destroyed by fire and war at the time Homer said it was.

The evidence is so strong that even those who refuse to believe the *Iliad* is anything but fiction reluctantly admit that there was a Troy in the place Homer said it was, that there was a Trojan War, and that the city was destroyed. If the *Iliad* is fiction, it is fiction based upon historical fact.

The account of Troy's fall in the Trojan War begins with Homer's *Iliad*, which marked the beginning of written Greek literature. However, the *Iliad* was apparently composed of numerous shorter oral poems that were current long before the legendary Homer wove them together into his famous epic. Many of these accounts appeared to differ greatly, and Homer chose or changed for his own purposes the original tales to fit his plot.

The *Iliad* was never intended to be a history of the fall of Troy. It is the story of one brief period in which the rage of one man almost brought doom to his companions. To tell this story Homer found it necessary to include much about the history of Troy. But even more was left out. However, Homer made allusions in passing to certain events, both in the *Iliad* and the *Odyssey*, that show he was aware of these other stories. Many of the stories were written down by writers who followed Homer. We know they did not invent them, although they may have distorted the originals, because of Homer's allusions to some of the events recorded.

Thus, in retelling the fall of Troy we can go further back than Homer to the mythological events that led to the tragedy at Troy VII-a.

Schliemann was often asked which was his favorite portion of Homer. He usually denied having a favorite, claiming it was all magnificent. But once he admitted that his favorite passage was the section in which King Priam calls Helen to the top of the Great Gate where he and the other old men are watching preparations for the single combat between Paris, Priam's son, and Achilles, the greatest of the attacking Greek warriors. Helen at this point is downcast because of all the trouble she has caused, but Priam tells her, "Come hither, dear child, and sit before me. . . . I hold thee not to blame; nay, I hold the gods to blame who brought on me the sorrowful war. . . ."

This theme that the war and all its destruction was caused by the gods and that men were swept into it by a destiny that could not be denied goes back to the very beginning of the pre-*Iliad* legends. In the *Cypria* (attributed to Stanius) we read:

> There was a time when countless men oppressed the surface of the earth. Zeus had pity and in his wisdom resolved to relieve the all-nurturing earth of men by causing the great Trojan War so that the multitude of deaths would empty the world of men.

Here we have a situation roughly comparable to the account of how Jehovah in the Bible decided to rid the earth of sinful men by sending the great flood in the time of Noah and his ark.

Once Zeus had determined to reduce the race of men by war, the situation only needed an incident to set it off. This came at the wedding feast the gods gave when the mortal Peleus and the immortal ocean goddess Thetis were married. It was not a happy marriage. In the *Iliad* Thetis complains to Hephaistos (the Greek Vulcan), the armorer of the gods, that no goddess in all Olympus had as many "grievous sorrows at the heart" as she because "Kronian Zeus chose me from among the sisters of the sea to enthrall me to a man, even Peleus, Aiakos' son, and with a man I endured wedlock sore against my will. Now lieth Peleus in his halls forespent with age."

Thetis had more troubles than just being married to a mortal who would grow old while she remained outwardly young. Other events were in motion that would bring about the death of her beloved son, Achilles, not yet born to her, and cause the bloody Trojan War through which Zeus sought to reduce the number of men on earth.

Unknown face found by Schliemann in the Trojan ruins. Archaeologists suggest it may be a later portrait of Priam or a religious figure.

During the wedding feast the goddess Discord threw a golden apple on the table before the assembled guests. On it were engraved the words "To the Fairest." As Discord had intended, the apple was claimed by the imperious Hera, wife of Zeus, by Athena, and by Aphrodite (Venus), because each in her individual egotism thought herself the fairest in Olympus.

They appealed to Zeus to settle the argument, but he was too sly to get embroiled in the fight. Also, he foresaw how the situation would lead to the destruction of the Trojans. For some reason not disclosed, Zeus favored the branch of Dardanus' family who had settled in the Mount Ida region and hated the branch under Ilos who had settled at Hissarlik. He slyly suggested that they take the quarrel to Paris, son of Priam of Troy, for he was a great judge of beauty.

Priam, after Heracles made him king of Troy, had married Hecuba, a Phrygian princess, and Paris was one of their sons. Before his birth, Hecuba dreamed that midwives took a burning torch from her body. Priam's soothsayers interpreted this as a foreshadowing of the burning of Troy through some future act of this unborn child. Priam, greatly disturbed, ordered that Paris be exposed on the slopes of Ida as soon as he was born. This was done, but the child was saved by shepherds. He grew up to be so beautiful and brave that men called him Alexandros (defender of men). Priam then welcomed Paris back into the family.

Paris married Oenone, daughter of the River Cebren, but continued to shepherd his flocks on Ida, for even kings' sons had to work in those days, even as kings' wives and daughters worked at the loom. Hermes, the messenger of the gods, flew to Ida to inform Paris that he had been chosen as judge of this classical beauty contest.

The Judgment of Paris has gripped the imagination of writers and artists, so that there are literally hundreds of versions of this famous incident. The version of Lucian, the satirist, is perhaps among the best, for Lucian laughed at the gods. In his account Paris first refused. He said that he was competent to choose which of three goats was the best, but he was no judge of human beauty.

However, Hermes persisted, and Paris agreed, provided that he could view the goddesses in private without their robes. They agreed, for each of them wanted to talk to their judge without the others' hearing.

Although all the artists who painted them preferred to show Paris with all three nude women, in Lucian they came one at a time. Hera was first. She promised that if Paris would give her the golden apple she would make him the most powerful man in the world and Lord of Asia. Athena came next. She promised Paris that she could make him the mightiest warrior of all times, a conqueror who would always win. Last to come was Aphrodite. As the goddess of love she understood Paris better than the others.

According to Lucian, Aphrodite said, "Paris, I think you must be the handsomest man in all Phrygia. You are too beautiful to be married to the dowdy girls of this land. You deserve a girl as beautiful as I am. Perhaps Helen. If she caught sight of you, she would give everything to become your devoted wife. Have you heard of Helen?"

Paris had not, but if she were as beautiful as Aphrodite, he was eager to hear of her. Aphrodite replied that Helen was the child born to Leda after she was visited by Zeus in the form of a swan. As befitted a child born in such circumstances, she was as beautiful as a swan and her skin was soft as a swan's down. She was so beautiful that even as a child of ten she was stolen by Theseus, King of Athens, for his wife. She was rescued and brought back to Sparta, where the first men of all Greece sued for her hand.

Helen was given to Menelaus, brother of Agamemnon, king of Mycenae, and he and Helen became rulers of Sparta.

Upon Aphrodite's promise that he could have this woman, fairest of all earth creatures, Paris impulsively shoved the golden apple into Aphrodite's hands. This naturally infuriated Hera and Athena and placed them on the side of those who hated Troy.

From other accounts we learn that Paris sailed for Sparta, where he was welcomed by Menelaus and Helen. Menelaus was then called to Crete on royal business, and while he was gone, Helen, influenced by Aphrodite, eloped with Paris. When Menelaus found his wife gone, he appealed to his brother Agamemnon for help in getting her back. Agamemnon, who appeared to have an overlord-ship over all the kings of Greek states, issued a call for war. The legends say the Greeks took ten years to prepare for the war, which in turn lasted for another ten years.

So much for legend and stories. How much of it is true? The excavations of Troy proved only that there was a Trojan War and that it occurred at the time Homer and the pre-Homeric legends say it did. As for the details, the classical Greeks believed in them. The great Greek historians, Herodotus and Thucydides, believed a lot of them. In addition, Herodotus found that both the Persians of whom he talked and the Egyptian priests he met also believed in the Trojan War. They did not, however, agree with Homer in all details.

The Egyptian priests told Herodotus that there had been a Helen and a Paris who stole her from a Menelaus. However, con-trary winds in the Aegean Sea drove Paris' ship to Egypt instead of Troy. The Egyptian king kept Helen, but drove out Paris. When the Greeks came to Troy, demanding the return of Helen, Priam an-swered truthfully that the Trojans did not have her. The Greeks, either disbelieving Priam or just seeking an excuse to sack the city, attacked anyway. After the fall of Troy, the Pharaoh restored Helen to Menelaus.

Herodotus says he believes this story, for Priam would never have allowed his city to fall just to keep Helen for the least worthy of his fifty sons. "The fact is," Herodotus says, "the Trojans did not give Helen back to Menelaus because they did not have her. . . . I do not hesitate to declare that the refusal of the Greeks to believe it was inspired by the gods, in order that the Trojans' utter destruction might plainly prove to mankind that sin is always visited by punish-ment."

Others would have us believe there was no Helen of Troy at all. The war, in their opinion, was economic. The Trojans may or may not have been pirates preying on commerce floating through the Black Sea. They were in a position to do so. Greece had to import much of her food. Herodotus pictures Xerxes, the Persian, watching loaded grain ships from the Black Sea area passing through the narrow Hellespont on their way to Attica.

It is also possible that Agamemnon had no real excuse at all and only wanted to extend his empire. Once the Greeks were rebuffed by the Trojans, it was a matter of national honor that they reduce the city to rubble. This was true regardless of the reason for the initial attack.

And so they fought for ten years. It was not a steady siege. They fought and then broke off to go pirating for supplies before returning for new assaults.

Thucydides, a better historian than Herodotus, said the Greek Mycenaean forces surpassed any of previous times, but were short of "modern efforts." By modern efforts he meant his own time, which was 460 to 400 B.C. He felt that the Trojan War was part of Greek expansion and that it went on so long the Greeks did not have sufficient money for supplies. This forced them to spend too much time in piracy. "This is what enabled the Trojans to stand them off for ten years," he insisted.

5

THE WRATH OF ACHILLES

The supreme account of the Trojan War is the *Iliad*, the epic poem attributed to the blind poet Homer. The *Iliad* is not in itself an account of the entire war. It deals in detail with forty-one days during the final year of the war. The story line revolves around the anger of the greatest of the Greek heroes, Achilles, and the tragic events that transpire because of his wrath.

The story is simply told. Nothing is obscure. The motivation and actions of each character stand out boldly. This simplicity has caused some critics to call the characters two-dimensional. They complain that there is no character development. The characters remain all through the story exactly as they entered it as far as their personalities are drawn.

This is hardly a valid criticism. The character of the men and women of the *Iliad* had already been molded. The epic begins at the end of the war, and nothing remains but for heroic people to face their destiny. We can understand each character and understand why that character acted as he did, even if we do not necessarily agree with him. Homer has shown us the very souls of these people.

As an example of this, consider the opening of the *Iliad*. The Greeks have just returned from a raiding party to obtain supplies.

Among the booty they bring back is the girl Chryseis, the beloved daughter of Chryses, an aged priest of Apollo. The story begins with the arrival of Chryses to plead for his daughter's return. Agamemnon, who has received the girl as his share of the raid, angrily refuses and threatens Chryses if the old man does not leave.

In despair Chryses prays to Apollo: "Hear me, god of the silver bow! . . . If ever I built a temple gracious in thine eyes, or if ever I burnt to thee fat thighs of bulls or goats, fulfill thou this my desire; let the Danaans pay by thine arrows for my tears."

Apollo hears and answers by bringing calamities upon the Greeks, who recognize that some god is interfering in the war. Achilles, the greatest hero among the Greeks, demands in council that they ask Calchas, their soothsayer, what caused the god's wrath. Calchas refuses unless Achilles guarantees his safety against one of their number whom he must criticize as the cause of their trouble with the god. Achilles agrees. Calchas then says that Apollo's wrath was due to the way Agamemnon, their leader, treated Apollo's priest. His wrath will not stop until the girl is restored to her father.

At this point Agamemnon shows the true character of his manhood under the heroic shell of his leadership. He reluctantly agrees to return Chryseis to her father, but insists that he will not be left without a prize. He demands Briséis, a girl who had been given to Achilles, in return for losing Chryseis.

Although he claims that he should not be deprived of a prize because he is the leader, his actions and words, directed at Achilles, definitely show that he is bitterly jealous of Achilles' fame as a warrior. While Achilles is furious at losing Briséis, whom he has promised to marry after they return to Greece, the action and words make it plain that Achilles is resentful of Agamemnon's position as leader while he, a greater warrior, must serve under the king of Mycenae.

Achilles accuses Agamemnon of holding back from battle while better men win for him. He threatens to withdraw from future fighting and take his followers, the Myrmidons, back to Thessaly.

Agamemnon replies contemptuously, "Yea, flee, if thy soul be set thereon. It is not I that beseech thee to tarry for my sake. I have others by my side to do me honor. Most hateful are thou to me of all kings!"

Achilles reaches for his sword, but he is restrained by Athena, who is invisible to all but Achilles. Nestor, the oldest of the kings supporting Agamemnon, tries to arbitrate the quarrel. Haughty Agamemnon refuses. He accuses Achilles of trying to take the leadership of the Greeks away from him. "He would be lord of all and king among all and captain to all!" Agamemnon cries.

Achilles, seething with rage, gathers his Myrmidons and goes back to his beached ships. His mother, the goddess Thetis (at whose wedding Discord brought the golden apple), comes to him. Achilles cries as he tells her how Agamemnon treated him so badly after all he had done on the battlefield. He begs his mother to ask Zeus to aid the Trojans so that Agamemnon and the other Greeks will realize how important Achilles is to success in battle.

Vase painting found by Schliemann at Mycenae shows a woman bidding farewell to soldiers going to war. Agamemnon's forces at Troy probably dressed like this.

Zeus owes Thetis a favor. He became king of the gods by deposing his father Cronos. The other gods then bound Zeus in an attempt to overthrow his rule, and Thetis loosened Zeus's bonds.

So begins the *Iliad*. At this point the narrative breaks into three separate but dependent stories. One, the story of Achilles' wrath, is an account of the hatred and rivalry between two strong men, and the tragedy that results from it.

The second story is an account of rivalry and hatred among the gods of Olympus. This story creates, so far as we know, Greek mythology. Just as the Judeo-Christian Bible has God creating man in His own image, Homer creates his gods in man's image. Zeus is an autocratic earth father transferred to Olympus with his nagging wife and his rebellious children and relatives. He is pictured as indecisive, underhanded, sometimes soft-hearted, and sometimes cruel.

The third story is that of Troy itself, with its hero Hector standing above all the others, from Olympus to Mycenae, in honor, dignity, and likability.

Oddly enough, the story of Achilles' wrath glorifies war and heroism, and it is easy to see why great military men from Caesar and Alexander to modern generals have delighted in it. But the Trojan account is a deeply moving antiwar story. The horror, brutality, and senseless slaughter are realistically depicted, along with the suffering. The farewell scene between Hector and his wife Andromaché, when both knew he is going to his death, is especially poignant. Then Homer makes it plain that the real villians of his triple-threaded story are the vain, jealous gods themselves.

In seeking Zeus's help to salve her mortal son's injured vanity, Thetis has to wait until she finds Zeus alone, because Hera, Zeus's wife, has hated the Trojans ever since Paris slighted her in awarding the golden apple to Aphrodite. Agamemnon receives a dream, inspired by Zeus, to attack Troy immediately. He musters all his soldiers, except the sulking Achilles and his men. The Trojans, led by the great Hector, came out to meet them on the Plain of Troy.

Instead of a battle, Paris challenged Menelaus to single combat between the two of them. If Paris wins, he will keep Helen. If

Menelaus wins, he will get Helen back, plus the treasure of Troy. In either case, the war will end. Both sides agree. Priam brings Helen to the tower atop the Scaean gate to watch the fight between her former husband and her new one.

Menelaus is winning when Aphrodite, repaying her debt to Paris, carries the loser off to Troy. The duel is declared won by Menelaus. This disturbs the gods who sided with the Trojans. Besides, Athena wants the fighting to continue. She persuades Pandarus of the Trojans to make a treacherous attack on Menelaus during the truce. Pandarus manages to wound the Greek. Agamemnon is outraged by this cowardly assault on his brother and orders the fighting resumed. "Many Trojans that day and many Acheans [Greeks] were laid side by side with their faces in the dust," Homer wrote.

The war continues by day, pausing at dusk for the men to rest through the night. Hera and Athena, fearing a Greek loss, prepare to join the fighting themselves. Zeus, seeing them from afar, sends a messenger with a threat to throw a thunderbolt at both of them if they enter the battle.

"Neither within the courses of ten years shall they heal themselves of the wounds my thunderbolts shall tear," he threatens. He condemns his daughter for defying him and complains of Hera, "It is ever her wont to thwart me, whate're I have decreed." Later in a family conference on Olympus, Zeus again threatens his wife and daughter if they join the battle.

The battle slaughter is enormous. The Trojans push the Greeks back toward their beached ships. Agamemnon now realizes how badly the Greeks need Achilles, for in this last attack the Trojans have come close to burning the Greek ships. He sends Odysseus to persuade Achilles to return to the battle, promising to return Briséis and to give Achilles heavy rewards in addition. The sulking hero, his pride still hurt, refuses.

Agamemnon, unable to sleep that night, goes to the tent of Nestor, seeking advice. Nestor persuades him to call a night council of his leaders. This results in Diomedes' and Odysseus' slipping into the Trojan camps as spies.

The battle is renewed the next day. The Trojans under Hector press forward. Again the Greek ships are in danger of being burned. The gods supporting the Greeks are frantic. Hera lulls Zeus to sleep so that Poseidon can aid Agamemnon. Hector is wounded, but his men close around him and carry him back to safety.

Zeus is furious when he awakens. He orders Apollo to restore Hector's health and threatens Hera with the direst punishment. She puts the blame on Poseidon. Zeus then foretells the future, saying that with his help Hector will push back the Achaeans and kill Patroclus, the friend of Achilles. Then he will allow the war to turn in the Greeks' favor and the Greeks will take "steep Ilios. But before that hour neither do I cease in my wrath, nor will I suffer any other of the Immortals to help the Danaans [Greeks] there, before I accomplish that desire of the son of Peleus [Achilles], as I promised him and confirmed the same with a nod of my head, on that day when the goddess Thetis clasped my knees, imploring me to honor Achilles."

In this statement Zeus shows that his heart is with the Greeks. He had been willing to slaughter many of them, however, in order to pay his deep debt to Thetis.

Patroclus, the great friend of Achilles, is in anguish at the defeats suffered by the Achaeans under Agamemnon. He keeps pleading with Achilles to take his Myrmidons back into battle. Achilles again refuses, but he does give Patroclus permission to join the battle. Patroclus is also given permission to wear Achilles' armor so that the Greeks will believe that Achilles is fighting with them and be inspired. In the ensuing battle Patroclus is slain by Hector.

Achilles is frantic with grief over his friend's death. His mother, Thetis, rushes to Hephaestus, the lame armorer of the gods, and persuades him to forge new armor for Achilles to replace that lost when Patroclus was slain. Homer describes the forging of the armor, particularly the magnificent shield, which is made of five layers of metal—two of bronze, two of tin, and one of gold. The outer gold layer is chased with scenes in relief.

Achilles dons his new armor and goes to make his peace with

Agamemnon. Agamemnon, echoing Priam's speech to Helen, blames Zeus for their troubles. Zeus, in Olympus, calls a council of the gods as events move toward their tragic conclusion. He tells them all they can join the fighting on whichever side they wish. The implication, however, is that it will do them no good, for the doom of Troy has already been foretold by Zeus.

"Meanwhile the whole plain was filled with men and horses," Homer relates. "And the earth rang with the feet of them as they rushed together in the fray. Two men far better than the rest were meeting in the midst of the hosts, eager for battle, Aeneas and noble Achilles." Aeneas is the leader of the Dardanian branch of the Trojans, who remained at Mount Ida when Ilios founded Troy on the mound of Hissarlik. We get the impression that Aeneas is not on the best of terms with Priam and his sons, but Aeneas, answering the call of blood, comes anyway to fight with his cousins against the Achaeans from Greece.

The gods, after their first participation in the battle, withdraw to watch from a hill after Poseidon suggests that they leave the fighting to men. They see Achilles about to kill Aeneas, and Poseidon suggests that it would be best to intervene again.

"Come let us guide Aeneas out of harm's way," he says, "lest the son of Cronos [Zeus] be wroth, if Achilles slay him; for it is appointed for Aeneas to escape, so that the race of Dardanos perish not without seed or sign."

Poseidon goes on to remark that Zeus loved Dardanus more than any of the other mortal children born of his earth mistresses, but hates the race of Priam. Therefore, it is Zeus's will that Aeneas should rule over the Trojans.

This portion of the *Iliad* is the bedrock upon which the Roman poet Vergil based his epic poem the *Aeneid*, which pictures Aeneas as the spiritual founder of Rome.

Poseidon goes into the battle, throws mist into Achilles' eyes, and in a mighty leap, carries Aeneas to the edge of the fray where he will face lesser warriors. Later Achilles and Hector face each other, but their personal conflict is indecisive. Achilles is like a madman, caught up in a blood lust that sweeps everything before him. The Trojans are driven back behind the walls of their city. Poseidon irritably complains that he helped build these very walls and was cheated of his wages by Priam's father.

Hector comes out to battle Achilles, who warns his fellow Greeks to shoot no arrows at the Trojan hero, for Achilles wants no doubt as to who killed Hector. Hector is afraid. He knows that Achilles, spurred by blood lust, is stronger than he is. He runs from Achilles, and three times they circle the walls of Troy. Achilles is unable to catch the fleet-footed Trojan.

Then the gods interfere again. Athena—vicious in her hatred of the Trojans—appears to Hector in the guise of one of his brothers, urging him to fight.

Hector is resolved. To Achilles he says, "No longer, son of Peleus, will I fly thee, as before I thrice ran round the great town of Priam. Now my heart biddith me stand up against thee. I will either slay or be slain."

He then says that if he kills Achilles he will return the dead hero's body to the Greeks for burial and asks Achilles to return his to Priam if it be he who is slain.

The Greeks of the time considered the lack of a proper burial the greatest calamity that could happen to a warrior. Earlier Priam showed this fear of unburial in a bitter lamentation when Hector decided to go out to meet Achilles face to face:

> Have compassion on me, the helpless one whom the father, Zeus, will bring to nought by a grievous doom in the path of old age, having seen full many ills, his sons perishing and his daughters carried away captive, and his chambers laid waste and infant children hurled to the ground in a terrible way, and his sons' wives dragged away.
>
> Myself then last of all at the street door will ravening dogs tear, when some one by stroke or throw of the sharp bronze has bereft my limbs of life—even the dogs I reared in my halls about my table and to guard my door, which then having drunk my blood, maddened at heart shall lie at the gateway

. . . when dogs defile the hoary head and hoary beard and the secret parts of an old man slain, this is the most piteous thing that can come upon hapless man.

Achilles is without pity, obsessed by his hatred of the Trojans. He refuses Hector's request and the fight begins. Hector gets a clear shot at Achilles with his spear, but Athena diverts the point. Hector has lost his one chance and is fatally speared by Achilles.

As he lies on the ground dying, he again asks Achilles to "give them home my body back again, that the Trojans and Trojans' wives give me my due of fire before my death [cremation]."

"Entreat me not, dog, by knees or parents," Achilles replies. "Would that my heart's desire could so bid me myself to carve and eat raw thy flesh. . . . Dogs and birds shall devour thee utterly."

Hector replies, "Verily I know thee and behold thee as thou art. . . . Truly is thy heart iron in thy breast." He predicts that Paris, aided by Apollo, will slay Achilles.

Achilles is not, nor was he ever, concerned with his own death. "For my death," he says to the dead body of his enemy, "I will accept it whensoever Zeus and the other immortal gods are minded to accomplish it."

The death of Hector fails to satisfy Achilles' wrath. He cuts the tendons of Hector's feet and, passing a rope through the cuts, drags the dead hero around the Greek camp. Priam and Hecuba, watching from the walls of Troy, weep for their dead son. Andromaché, Hector's wife, is hysterical. The Trojan women wail a Greek tragic chorus behind her.

Achilles throws Hector's body in the open for dogs to devour, but Aphrodite personally keeps them back. In the meantime, Achilles arranges funeral games for Patroclus. The Greeks traditionally play such games at the funeral of a great hero. Patroclus' body is burned, after which the games begin. The first, a chariot race, is described by Homer in detail. General Lew Wallace, who admired the *Iliad*, may well have gotten the idea of the great chariot race in his *Ben Hur* from the wild race in Homer.

After the games a mound tomb is built over Patroclus' charred bones. Achilles pulls Hector's body around the tomb. In Olympus there is an argument among the gods. Some wish to steal Hector's body and return it to Priam. Athena, Hera, and Poseidon object strenuously. The death of Hector has not erased their vicious hatred of all Trojans. Apollo reproaches them all for disrespect to a dead hero, and Zeus finally intercedes. He sends Thetis to tell her son Achilles that the lord of Olympus is angry at his refusal to return Hector's body for a decent funeral. Zeus also sends word to Priam to take presents to Achilles as payment for Hector's corpse.

When Priam meets his son's killer, Achilles is strangely civil. He readily agrees when Priam asks for a ten-day truce so that Hector can be given a proper mourning period before cremation.

And so, "when the tenth morn rose with light for men, then bare they forth brave Hector, weeping tears, and on a lofty pyre they laid the dead man, and thereon cast fire."

Later the burned bones are placed in a golden urn and covered with a purple robe before being placed in a shallow grave which is covered with close-set stones and then heaped with earth.

"Thus held they funeral for Hector tamer of horses."

And so ends the *Iliad* with the Trojan War still unresolved.

The *Iliad* is one of the supreme literary achievements of all time. It has been criticized for some disunity, for unnecessary repetition, for lack of character development because the people depicted do not undergo drastic changes, and even for the choice of the theme. One critic—Gilbert Murray—claimed that the unifying theme of the *Iliad*, the wrath of Achilles, was a "second rate subject." Almost all critics point out that the writing itself consists of many stock phrases that evidently came from the wandering minstrels of the day. It is, in fact, a collection of grand clichés. Others complain that the introduction of the gods is poor plotting, it being basic to modern writing that a hero wins or loses on his own abilities.

All such criticisms can be refuted. In the first place, the *Iliad* was probably composed by Homer, although no one knows for sure, in the seventh century B.C. and first transcribed to paper in the sixth century B.C. by writers. It was originally composed for the still barbaric people of the heroic age. Perhaps it was refined as it was retold orally and perhaps it gained humanity before it was written down. We must not lose sight of the fact that the *Iliad* is 2,700 years old. That anything that ancient still holds up so well both artistically and emotionally is remarkable.

The epic has been described as "the bible of Greece." The Greeks of the classical age considered it the ultimate masterpiece, and the greatest writers of the period drew themes and inspiration from it. Occasionally there was a sorehead. Plato complained that if Homer was so great why was there not a Homeric philosophy? He expected a blueprint, like his own *Republic*, for an idealized way of life.

That is hardly fair, although one hesitates to argue with Plato. A personal philosophy for the development of an honorable man is deeply engraved in every line of the *Iliad*. Homer does not spell this out in dull discourse and argument. He shows it to us in the actions of his tragic characters.

A leader should be just in his treatment of his followers. Homer shows us in Agamemnon what happens when he is not. The Greek leader's jealousy and arrogant treatment of Achilles leads to tragedy.

A follower must be a member of the team. He must put his own desires below the welfare of the group. This is true whether the group is an army fighting Troy, a baseball team, a Communist cell, or followers of a religious faith. Achilles let his pride stand in opposition to the welfare of his fellow warriors simply because he hated one man. Hundreds died because of it.

Similarly in the actions of other characters we see the disastrous results of men failing to live up to the moral standards of their times. We see this in the personal tragedies of the soldiers who died needlessly and in the effect it had upon innocent victims like Hector's wife, Andromaché, his infant son, his mother, and his father.

One of the amazing things about the *Iliad* is its realism, remarkable for such an early age in literature. Tradition claims that Homer was blind, and he may have been, but the blindness must have struck him late in life, for the *Iliad* is jammed with touches of realism that only one who had seen and been there could have included.

This does not mean that he was at Troy. The *Iliad* was composed at least four hundred years after the fall of the city, but Homer knew his Greek armies, and he includes details that show how well

An artist's conception of Homer stands in front of a souvenir shop just outside the ruins. No one knows what Homer really looked like. The sign in Turkish reads: "Homer: A Child of Anatolia, the Father of the World's Poetry."

he knew them. Such things as how the ships were moored, how food was prepared, and how the chariots were hitched all add believability to the story.

Nor are these realistic details restricted to military matters. There is a very human touch to the scene where Hector, sure he will die in battle, bids farewell to Andromaché and his infant son. The infant is frightened by the waving horsehair plume on Hector's helmet, for he has never before seen his father in armor. Hector laughs and removes the helmet before taking his son in his arms. Little human touches like this help point up the tragedy.

Since Troy is better known through Homer than through history, a major question is, how true to history is the *Iliad*? Some, like Schliemann in the beginning, look upon it as absolute fact. Others, especially in the years before Schliemann uncovered the ruins, have dismissed the *Iliad* as pure fiction. Today the consensus is somewhere between the two extremes. It is historical fiction and no one can say where history stops and fiction starts.

This much is fact: There was a Troy. There was a Trojan War. The attackers came from Mycenae, and tradition calls the leader Agamemnon. No one believes that a girl named Helen was the reason for the war, although Herodotus, the Egyptian priests, and the Persians believed that a Helen was abducted.

Also, Homer was guilty of anachronisms. He has his characters using iron swords, but excavations in Troy show that Troy VII-a was in the Middle Aegean Bronze Age. Much of his description is based upon the culture of his own day and not that of the Trojan War period. On the other hand, an embossed gold cup that Schliemann found in Mycenae is almost perfectly like one described in Homer. There is obviously much truth in the Iliad.

Much argument has been waged about whether Homer ever saw the Troad. Definite proof exists that he either personally walked through the Troad or knew somebody who did. This proof is in the fact that his geographic descriptions were so accurate that Schliemann was able to use them to determine that Hissarlik was the real Troy.

As for the traditional oral matter that Homer used, we have no reason to discount it all. Perhaps the story was made bigger than life, as Homer turned the small city of Troy into a much larger place by the use of poetic license, but there is plenty of evidence to show that many traditional tales have retained a basis of truth.

6

THE FALL OF TROY

Aeschylus, who wrote at least six plays based upon the Trojan legends, called them "slices from Homer's banquet." He was not the only writer of the past and present who dined at Homer's literary table. Hundreds of them wrote directly upon Trojan themes, and the number would be in the thousands if we include those who have made allusions to the great city and its tragic inhabitants.

Some of the most famous stories about the fall of Troy come from writers who followed Homer. The famous Wooden Horse, the love affair between Achilles and the Amazon Queen Penthesilea, the Ethiopian king Memnon, the return of Helen to Menelaus, the escape of Aeneas from burning Troy, and the bitterly tragic cycle dealing with the fate of Agamemnon upon his return to Mycenae are all found in works that were written after the *Iliad*.

In some cases the authors took references in the *Iliad* and blew them into full-fledged imaginary adventures. One particular example is Poseidon's prediction that Aeneas would rule over the Trojans. Vergil based his *Aeneid* upon this fragment from Homer. In the *Cypria*, ascribed to Stasinus, who may have lived shortly after Homer, many of the references to Troy before the Greek attack have been welded into a complete history that begins with Zeus's decision to reduce mankind, continues through the Judgment of Paris, and stops where the *Iliad* begins.

The *Iliad* ends with Hector's funeral; Homer records the actual fall of Troy only in an account sung by a blind bard (a self-portrait?) to Odysseus years later. The Trojan Horse account comes, not from Homer, but from. *The Sack of Troy*, ascribed to Arctinus (sixth century B.C.?), from *The Little Iliad*, ascribed to Lesches (sixth century B.C.), and from *The Fall of Rome* by Quintus of Smyrna (fourth century B.C.), among others.

By piecing together the various accounts, we arrive at the following composite story of events that come after those described in the *Iliad*.

After the truce for Hector's funeral, the fighting resumes, and the Trojans, dispirited by Hector's death, retreat behind their walls. Friends come to help them. One is Penthesilea, the Amazon, who left Thrace after accidentally killing her sister Hippolyte. Penthesilea is as beautiful as a goddess and fights like a tiger. She inspires the Trojans, who regain some of their lost spirit. In her first fight she kills a dozen men. Then she confronts Achilles and arrogantly tells him that her might is greater than that of any man.

When Achilles laughs at her, Penthesilea becomes enraged. She hurls her spear at him and misses. Achilles taunts her and then drives his own spear into her left breast. When he sees her lying dead in the dirt, Achilles realizes that he has fallen in love with the beautiful and bold woman warrior. (Thorwalsen carved a touching relief of Achilles lifting the dead Amazon from the dirt.)

One of the Greeks taunts Achilles for his reaction to the girl's death, and Achilles kills the man with a blow from his fist. He personally carries Penthesilea's corpse to the Trojans for proper burial as a heroic warrior. The Greeks mourn her as much as the Trojans. She was an enemy, but they respect her for her bravery.

The next to come to Troy's aid is Memnon, king of Ethiopia. (Ethiopian meant "burnt skin" to the Greeks, who applied the name to all dark-skinned people. It did not refer to the present nation of Ethiopia, but probably to Merowe in the present Sudan.) Memnon is a giant of a man who delights in battle. He and his Ethiopians cause havoc in the ranks of the Greeks before he is killed. Then, to the astonishment of both the Greeks and the Trojans, Memnon's grieving mother, the goddess of Dawn, sends the wind to pick up his body and take it away, along with all his Ethiopians.

Fate is now closing in on Achilles. According to a legend that sometimes figured in the Trojan cycle and sometimes did not, Thetis had dipped him in the River Styx, which separates earth from Hades, to make him invulnerable to all weapons. However, his heel, by which she held him, did not penetrate the water, and it was the one spot where he could be injured. Here he is struck by an arrow as he approaches the Scaean Gate of Troy. Writers differ on who shot the arrow. Some say Paris; some say Apollo; others say it was Paris guided by Apollo. In any event, Achilles is struck by the poison dart in the only place where he can be hurt, giving rise to the adage of the "Achilles' heel."

With Achilles dead, Agamemnon despairs of ever winning the war. At this point, spurred by Athena, the Greeks hit upon a trick. They will pretend to sail away, leaving behind a giant wooden horse in which selected Greek warriors will hide to spring out on the Trojans when they get the chance. The story of the Wooden Horse is one of the most famous connected with the Troy cycle of stories. Homer's version is in the *Odyssey*, and since the story is related by a blind bard, it gives a picture of the way Homer must have sung the *Iliad*. It is therefore worth quoting almost in its entirety.

Odysseus is prevented by the gods from returning immediately to his home when the war ends. After years of wandering, he comes to the court of King Alcinous. No one recognizes him, but his bearing proclaims him a person of consequence, and he is entertained as befits royalty. In the course of the feast Alcinous says:

> Call the bard, Demodocus, for surely God has granted him exceeding skill in song, to cheer us in whatever way his soul is moved to sing. . . .
>
> The page drew near, leading the honored bard. The muse had greatly loved him, and had given him good and ill. She

took away his eyesight but gave him delightful song. Ponton-
ous [his page] placed for Demodocus among the feasters a
silver-studded chair, backed by a lofty pillar, and hung his
tuneful lyre on its peg above his head. And the page showed
Demodocus how to reach it with his hands. . . .

Food and drink are placed in front of the blind bard, and after
he has eaten, Homer tells us:

The muse impelled the bard to sing men's glorious deeds, a lay
whose fame was then as wide as the sky. He sang the strife of
Odysseus with Pelian Achilles—how once they quarreled at
the gods' high feast with furious words, and Agamemnon, king
of men, rejoiced in spirit when the bravest of the Achaeans
quarreled. . . .

Odysseus hides his head under his cloak so that the others
cannot see his tears as Demodocus sings on of the glorious deeds of
the men who fought in the Trojan war. When the song ends the
feasters and their guest go out to play games, and after the games,
they eat again. Then:

The page drew near, leading the honored bard, Demodocus, beloved of all, and seated him among those feasting.
Then wise Odysseus, cutting a slice of saddle from out a
white-toothed boar, the rich fat on its side, said, "Page, set
before Demodocus this piece of meat, that he may eat and that
I may pay him homage. Of all on earth bards meet respect and
honor, because the muse has taught them song. . . ."
He spoke, and the page bore the food and put it in the
hands of Demodocus. After they had eaten, then to Demodocus said wise Odysseus:
"Demodocus, I praise you beyond all mortal men. . . .
With perfect truth you sing the lot of the Achaeans, all that
they did and bore, the whole Achaean struggle, as if yourself
were there, or you had heard the tale from one who was. Pass
on then now, and sing the building of the wooden horse, made

by Epeius with Athena's aid, which royal Odysseus once conveyed into the Trojan citadel—a thing of craft, filled full of men, who by its means sacked Ilios. And if you now relate the tale in its due order, forthwith I will declare to all mankind how bounteously God gave to you a wondrous power of song."

So he spoke. Then Demodocus, stirred by the muse, began and showed his skill in song. He started the story where some Argives [Greeks], boarding the well-beached ships, were setting sail, and spreading fire through the camp. Others still, under famed Odysseus, lay in the assembly of the Trojans all hidden inside the wooden horse, for the Trojans had dragged it to their citadel.

It stood there, while long and impatiently the Trojans argued about it. Three plans were considered with favor, to split the hollow trunk with axes, to drag it to the heights and hurl it on the rocks, or to spare the giant horse as an offering to the gods. And thus at last it was to end. For it was fated that they should perish so soon as their city should enclose the enormous wooden horse, where the Argive chiefs were lying, bearing to the Trojans death and doom.

Homer merely sketches the story of the Wooden Horse and omits entirely the account of Helen imitating the voices of the wives of the Greeks hidden inside and the story of Laocoön, the suspicious priest. Helen's attempt to trick the Greeks into revealing their presence is not too well known, but Laocoön is world famous because of the magnificient Roman statue of him and his sons fighting Poseidon's serpents, and because of the oil masterpiece by El Greco on the same theme.

The classic story of the Wooden Horse and Laocoön is in Vergil's *Aeneid*, the story of Aeneas of the Dardanian branch of the Trojans.

According to this story, when the Greeks sail away, the Trojans do not know what to make of the giant wooden horse left behind on the beach. One Greek, Sinon, has volunteered to stay with the horse. He tells the Trojans that he has been badly treated by the

Troy without a Wooden Horse is unthinkable. This one was being constructed in 1975 at the edge of the ruins. The pagoda on its back serves as a lookout tower where visitors can view the site. The scaffolding makes it look as it might have appeared when the Greeks built it at Odysseus' suggestion.

Greeks and has deserted them. He is put to torture to test his truthfulness, but sticks to his story and is finally believed. He tells the Trojans that the horse was left behind as a votive offering to Athena. The Trojans then knock down a portion of the wall to drag the horse (which is wheeled) into the city.

Earlier Paris had been hit by a poisoned arrow. Dying, he was told that he would recover if Oenome, the wife he abandoned for Helen, forgave him. He died before this could happen (Quintus of Smyrna's version). Shepherds built a funeral pyre for his body and Oenome threw herself into the fire. Mountain nymphs, who remembered the youthful Paris, danced sadly around the fire.

In the *Aeneid*, Laocoön, a priest of Apollo, warns his fellow Trojans that the wooden horse is a trick, speaking the famous line that has since become an adage, "I fear Greeks bearing gifts!"

He strikes the side of the horse with his spear to prove that it is hollow. The gods who hate Troy fear that Laocoön will discover the Greeks hidden inside.

Poseidon sends two giant serpents to seize Laocoön's sons. When the father rushes to their aid, he is likewise caught in their coils. "He the while strains his hands to burst the knots," Vergil wrote, "his fillets steeped in gore and black venom; the while he lifts heaven with hideous cries, like the bellowing of a wounded bull."

The famous statue of Laocoön in the Vatican, Rome, shows him at this awful moment. Laocoön is heroic in size as he struggles with the serpents. His head is thrown back and his mouth is open, crying out. On each side of him, the smaller figures of his sons also struggle with the snakes. The marble group was carved about 50 B.C., although this one is thought to be a copy of a lost original. According to Pliny, the original was carved by three sculptors, Agesandros, Polydoros, and Athenodoros of Rhodes. The three figures and the snakes were carved from a single block of marble.

The death of Laocoön is ignored by the people of Troy. They assume that it was a just punishment because he struck Athena's Wooden Horse with his spear. Cassandra, Priam's prophetess daughter, goes about crying that doom is coming to the city, but everyone is too overjoyed at the ending of the long war to pay attention to her. Helen, in the meantime, has married Deiphobus, another son of Priam. Apparently only a few hours have elapsed between Paris' death and her remarriage.

When the tired Trojans cease celebrating and go to their beds,

Sinon releases the hidden Greeks from the belly of the Wooden Horse, and the Greeks, who only pretended to sail away, come back. They pour through the broken wall (torn down to get the Wooden Horse into the city) while the Greeks from the horse attack the sleeping Trojans.

Blood soaks the ground. Fire sweeps through the city and walls crumble under the heat. Neoptolemus, son of Achilles, whom Odysseus brought to the battleground after his father was slain, kills King Priam and dashes the body of infant Astyanax, Hector's son, from the walls.

At the height of the destruction, Aeneas, carrying his aged father on his back and leading his son by the hand, escapes from the doomed city in fulfillment of Zeus's declaration that he would survive to rule over the Trojans.

Helen's actions at the fall of Troy are controversial. There are varying accounts. She claims later that she always wanted to return to Greece, but was prevented from doing so. When Telemachus, son of Odysseus, visits Sparta in search of his lost father, he is entertained by Menelaus and Helen. Helen, in the presence of her husband, tells how she penetrated Odysseus' disguise when he came into Troy as a spy. She says she aided him in getting away.

"My soul was glad," Homer (in the *Odyssey*) has her tell Telemachus, "for my heart already turned toward going home again, and I mourned the blindness Aphrodite brought when she lured me thither from my native land and bade me leave my daughter, my chamber, and my husband—a man who lacks for nothing in mind or body."

Of course, here Helen is speaking in the presence of her wronged husband, and her truthfulness may well be suspect. Quintus of Smyrna claimed that Menelaus, when he found Helen in a room in the burning city, drew his sword to kill her. Instead he was stricken by her goddesslike beauty and forgot all the wrongs she had done him.

Then, as other Greeks approached, Menelaus drew his sword to trick them into believing he intended to kill Helen. Agamemnon objected to further punishment. He laid all the blame on Paris, who had paid for his crime with his death. Menelaus was very pleased to agree with his brother.

The *Little Iliad*, attributed to Lesches, tells a similar tale. Helen in his version carefully prepares her toilet to bring out the full impact of her beauty before she confronts her wronged husband. When Menelaus sees her, he drops his sword. The *Little Iliad* is a lost manuscript and exists only in a synopsis and in fragments preserved in other writings.

Euripides, in *The Trojan Women*, a play first presented in 412 B.C., draws a pathetic and emotional picture of the plight of the survivors. The play opens with Poseidon and Athena agreeing to punish the Greeks by turning their homeward voyages into disasters. Athena's attitude is strange, for it was her vicious hatred that led to Troy's destruction. While Euripides does not say so, the reason her anger has now turned against the Greeks she previously aided may have been an act of Ajax the Lesser. Polyxena, the virgin youngest daughter of Priam and Hecuba, took refuge in Athena's temple at the fall of Troy. Ajax found her there and attempted to rape her. Polyxena threw her arms about the statue of Athena and it toppled over as Ajax tried to pull her away from it. The other Greeks were so horrified at the sacrilege to Athena's statue that they threatened to stone Ajax to death.

Athena watched the desecration of her temple, but took no action. However, considering how easily her feelings were upset, this could well have been the reason for her turning against the Greeks. Euripides mentions Poseidon's surprise at how readily his niece agrees to cause the Greeks troubles on their way home.

After the gods plot their malicious interference, Hecuba, widow of Priam, laments the fate of the Trojans. Then Talthybius, a Greek herald, enters to report that Agamemnon has taken Cassandra as his concubine. Polyxena, Priam's virgin daughter, has been sacrificed on Achilles' tomb by the dead hero's son, who claimed his father's ghost demanded it. Neoptolemus was to receive Hector's widow Andromaché as his prize, and Odysseus was to receive Hecuba.

At this point Cassandra enters, holding aloft a burning torch. The Greek chorus accompanying the actors cries that she has gone mad as she dances and prays that Agamemnon will take her with him to Mycenae so that she can cause the death of him and all his family.

Andromaché enters, riding a chariot filled with the spoils of war that the Greeks are taking from the burning city. She is distraught, and Hecuba tries to comfort her. Hecuba advises Andromaché to try and win the love of Neoptolemus, to whom she has been given as war booty, in hopes that he will thus spare the infant Astyanax. They are interrupted by the herald, who tells them the Greeks cannot permit a son of Hector to live. As Andromaché is led away to witness the child's death, the Greek chorus of Trojan women begins wailing again.

Menelaus strides in, demanding that Helen be dragged before him to receive her punishment. Hecuba, her hatred centering on Helen, urges Menelaus to slay his faithless wife before her fatal beauty destroys his resolve. Menelaus is unable to do so. He finds an excuse to postpone any action by saying it is right that Helen be taken back to Sparta, where relatives of those who died in the fighting can join in the pleasure of stoning her to death.

Helen, dignified in her hour of supreme peril, demands the right to speak in her own defense. She rejects responsibility for the Trojan War. She blames Priam and Hecuba for not killing Paris after the oracle predicted that he would bring disaster to Troy. She also blames Aphrodite for promising her to Paris in return for the golden apple.

Hecuba interrupts, claiming all the trouble was caused by Helen's sins. She claims that Helen could have escaped or even killed herself if she had really been forced to stay in Troy. Helen drops to her knees before Menelaus. Hecuba also kneels before him, begging for Helen's death. Menelaus replies that he will stand by his original decision. Helen will be taken back to Greece. She is led away as the herald returns, bearing the dead body of Astyanax on his dead father's shield. He tells Hecuba that Andromaché, as she was led to the Greek ships, begged that her son should be returned to his grandmother for proper burial.

The death of her grandson, following that of her husband, sons, and daughters, is too much for the queen of Troy. Wailing piteously, she tries to throw herself into the flames of the burning city. She is dragged back and led with the remaining captive women to the ships for transport to slavery in Greece. As the women wail, the walls of Troy can be heard crashing in the background.

7

AFTER THE FALL OF TROY

The *Iliad* is an unfinished story, and it is natural that other writers should try to supply the missing parts. Later bards and authors did not stop just with taking the story on to the fall of the city. The characters had become so familiar that audiences and readers wanted to know all that happened to them.

"Sequels are never equals," according to playwright George S. Kaufman. One can cite hundreds of sequels to the *Iliad* that bears this out. However, Homer himself wrote his own sequel in the *Odyssey*. While Greeks of the classical period preferred the *Iliad* to the later epic, today the *Odyssey* is the more widely read.

It is the story of the wanderings of Odysseus on his ten-year trip home to Ithaca. When the epic opens, all the surviving heroes of the Trojan War have returned home except Odysseus. His wife, Penelope, is besieged by suitors who want to marry her. Telemachus, Odysseus' son, goes to Sparta to ask Menelaus if he has any knowledge of the lost hero. He finds Menelaus living with Helen, whom he has forgiven, but the king of Sparta confesses to Telemachus that he is not a happy man.

Homer has Menelaus saying, "Through many woes and wanderings I brought in my ships, and I was eight years on the way.

Cyprus, Phoenicia, Egypt, I wandered over." This accords with the agreement of Poseidon and Athena to make it difficult for the Greeks to return home.

Then Menelaus confesses:

> "While I was gathering there much wealth and wandering on [presumably pirating], a stranger slew my brother [Agamemnon] while off his guard, by stealth, and through the craft of his [Agamemnon's] cursed wife. Here too I have no joy as lord of my possessions.
>
> "But from your fathers you would have heard that tale, whoever they may be; for great was my affliction, and desolate my house which stood fair and stored with many blessings. Would I were here at home with but the third part of my wealth, and they were safe today who fell on the plain of Troy, far off from grazing Argos! But no! and for them all I often grieve and mourn while sitting in my halls.
>
> "Now with a sigh I ease my heart, then check myself. Soon comes a surfeit of benumbing sorrow. Yet in my grief it is not all I so much mourn as one alone, who makes me loathe my sleep and food when I remember him; for no Achaean met the contests that Odysseus met and won. And still on him it was appointed woe should fall, and upon me a ceaseless pain because of him."

Odysseus of the many wiles, however, is not dead. Contrary winds blow his homeward-bound ship far off course. He and his crew sack a city and then are blown to the island of the Lotus Eaters, where they almost succumb to sloth. Adventure follows adventure in the land of the Cyclops, the island of Aeolia, and then the men become captives of the enchantress Circe. After that Odysseus passes through new dangers and adventures before becoming captive of the nymph Calypso, but she reluctantly releases him on orders from Zeus.

Odysseus next goes to the court of King Alcinous of Phaeacia. He is welcomed as a stranger, but betrays his connection with the Trojan War by weeping when the blind bard Demodocus sings of the battle. Urged by Alcinous, Odysseus tells of his adventures since leaving Troy. Included is an account of Odysseus' visit to Hades, where he meets the shades of those who fell at Troy. Among them is Achilles. Odysseus says, "During your lifetime, we Argives gave you equal honor with the gods. Now you are a king among the dead. Do not grieve at having died, Achilles." To which the unhappy hero replies, "Do not mock death, glorious Odysseus. It is better to be the servant of a stranger than to be the ruler over all these who are dead and gone."

When Troy fell, fires were lighted on mountaintops to carry the victory news back to Mycenae. Clytemnestra, Agamemnon's queen, was not pleased by the news. In the opening of the *Iliad* Agamemnon reveals that he and his wife are not getting along well. He says that he prefers the captive girl Chryseis to his wife. Clytemnestra feels much the same about him, and she has taken Aegisthus, an enemy of Agamemnon, for her lover while her husband was away at war.

At the Hades meeting, the shade of Agamemnon reveals to Odysseus what happened when he returned home with Cassandra as his slave:

> It was Aegisthus, plotting death and doom, who slew me. He was aided by my accursed wife. . . . Saddest of all was the cry of Cassandra, Priam's daughter, whom crafty Clytemnestra slew as I on the ground lifted my hands and clutched my sword in dying.

Later Odysseus returns to Ithaca, where he fights and kills his wife's suitors. Then he lives happily ever after—the only one of the ill-fated people who fought at Troy who does find final happiness.

The classic version of Agamemnon's story is a trilogy by Aeschylus, first presented in 458 B.C. The three individual plays are called *Agamemnon*, *The Libation Bearers*, and *The Furies*.

In *Agamemnon*, the house of Atreus, the king of Mycenae, comes under a curse that is carried over to his sons, Agamemnon, ruler of Mycenae, and Menelaus, king of Sparta. When Helen was abducted by Paris, Menelaus had asked for his brother's aid, but the sea winds were contrary, and Agamemnon, in answer to oracular advice, had sacrificed his daughter Iphigenia to the gods.

Agamemnon's wife, Clytemnestra, has vowed revenge and made common cause with Aegisthus, whose father was wronged by Atreus, starting the curse that has continued to pursue Atreus' sons.

When the Trojan War ends Agamemnon returns, bringing with him his new mistress, Cassandra, who has already foretold Agamemnon's doom. Now, remaining outside in a chariot after Agamemnon has entered the palace, Cassandra, prophetess of doom, tells listeners that Clytemnestra will murder Agamemnon. She then goes into the palace.

Shortly thereafter spectators outside hear Agamemnon's death cry. Clytemnestra appears in the door with a bloody sword, claiming that she has killed her husband and his Trojan slave. There is an uproar from the citizenry, and Clytemnestra angrily defends herself.

Aegisthus claims his part in the murder was honest justice, because, years before, Atreus killed his two younger brothers and fed their flesh to their father, who ate it without knowing it.

Some claim that Agamemnon's absent son, Orestes, will avenge his father's death, and the play ends with the guilty pair defying the gods themselves.

In *The Libation Bearers*, the second play in the trilogy, Orestes, Agamemnon's son, returns to discover what has happened. He meets his sister, Electra, at their father's tomb, and prays to Agamemnon's ghost to give him strength to kill his mother and her lover, Aegisthus. Electra reminds him of the curse upon their house. She says she welcomes the coming of her own fate.

Orestes goes to the palace in disguise. He kills Aegisthus and then strikes Clytemnestra with the sword still dripping with Aegisthus' blood.

Orestes displays the bodies to the people of Mycenae. He then prays to Apollo. Although the double murders were something he had to do because it was right that his father should be avenged, he realizes that he must suffer for killing his own mother, regardless of her own bloody guilt. His punishment comes in the form of the

Furies, three terrible female spirits who pursue those whose crimes are unpunished. He goes mad under their vicious attack.

In *The Furies*, the concluding play in the trilogy, Orestes goes to Delphi, the great oracle of Apollo, seeking help. The Pythoness (the female who delivers the oracles) asks him to leave because the Furies are profaning the temple of Apollo. Apollo, feeling sympathy for the bedeviled man, puts the Furies to sleep so that Orestes can get some rest himself. He then tells the unhappy young man to visit the temple of Pallas Athena in Athens and seek absolution for his crime there.

Clytemnestra's ghost arouses the sleeping Furies so they can hound her son again, but Apollo orders the Furies to leave Orestes alone. They accuse the god of being the cause of the murders of Clytemnestra and Aegisthus. Apollo admits that he urged Orestes to avenge his father, whereupon the Furies claim that matricide, the murder of his mother by Orestes, is a far worse crime than her part in the slaying of Agamemnon and Cassandra.

Apollo agrees to let Athena judge Orestes, but she refuses and selects some judges. Orestes asks why he is being tried when his mother was not. He is told that he killed a blood relative in his mother, but that she did not, for neither her husband nor Cassandra was related to her by blood.

Then Apollo, acting as a defense attorney for Orestes, insists that a mother can never be the true parent, since it is the father who plants the seed. He defends this theory by pointing out that a family's descent is traced through the father's side. Therefore, Orestes is not guilty of slaying a blood kin. The judges agree, and although many people condemn their judgment, Athena accepts it and Orestes is freed. The Furies retire.

Pausanias (second century B.C.) visited Mycenae and wrote that the people of Mycenae buried Clytemnestra and Aegisthus outside the city walls because of their unworthiness. A graveyard was uncovered in the indicated area and is pointed out today as the supposed graves of the two. It will be recalled that a review of Pausanias' account led Schliemann to find the Mycenean graves and the great treasure he mistakenly called Agamemnon's.

Euripides and Sophocles also used the tragedy as a basis for their work. Sophocles, in his *Electra*, excuses Orestes' murder of his mother as being justified by Apollo's command. In that play the Furies do not pursue him, and a Greek chorus declares that the curse of the House of Atreus has been lifted by his bloody act.

Euripides also called his play *Electra*. It was first presented in 413 B.C. After the murder of Agamemnon, the guilty Clytemnestra and Aegisthus force Electra to marry an old peasant. They fear that if

Part of the circle of stones that surrounds the shaft graves of Mycenae where Schliemann found the golden masks.

she marries a young and ambitious man, he might have ideas about revenge and try to seize the throne of Mycenae himself.

Orestes, who was sent away to protect him from Aegisthus, secretly returns and meets his sister Electra. She urges him to slay Aegisthus and their mother. Orestes and his friend Pylades go in disguise to meet Aegisthus, while Electra sends word to Clytemnestra that she has given birth to a baby.

Aegisthus is sacrificing a calf to the nymphs when Orestes kills him with a blow in the back. They carry the corpse to Electra's hut, where she curses it. Now Clytemnestra approaches, and Orestes, faced with murdering his mother, loses heart. Electra urges him on, pointing out that their mother's death was prophesied by the oracle of Apollo at Delphi. Orestes goes ahead with the murder and then moans in distress. Electra feels both pride and shame.

The Dioscuri, twin sons of Zeus, appear to Electra and Orestes, but instead of condemning the two, they blame Apollo. They also decree that Electra should be taken from her aged peasant husband and married to Orestes' friend, Pylades. Orestes is to be pursued by the Furies until he can be freed by a trial before Athena in Athens.

Many writers who touched on the Trojan legend were concerned about the fate of Helen. In Homer's version, told in the *Odyssey*, she lived out her life quietly with her bitter husband.

Some writers went out of their way to find excuses for her. In the sixth century B.C. Stesichorus wrote a choral poem, *Palinode*, in which he claimed that the real Helen went to Egypt and that it was a phantom created by Hera that Paris took to Troy. Except for the phantom, this is somewhat like the story that Herodotus, the Greek historian, got from Egyptian priests. They claimed that Paris and Helen were shipwrecked on the Egyptian coast. The Pharaoh kept her prisoner while sending Paris back to Troy. When Priam told the Greeks that he did not have Helen, he was telling the truth. The Greeks refused to believe him and attacked Troy anyway. After the fall of the city the Egyptian king gave Helen back to Menelaus. This story was related to Herodotus as the truth and not as a literary invention.

Euripides, in his play *Helen*, first presented in 412 B.C., follows Stesichorus. The play opens with Helen a prisoner in Egypt, where Pharaoh is determined to marry her. She has been taken to Egypt by Hermes on orders of Hera, who has made a phantom Helen for Paris to steal. Hera has played this malicious trick because of resentment at Paris for giving the golden apple to Aphrodite and accepting Helen's love as his bribe.

The play portrays Helen as blameless. Menelaus, with the phantom Helen he believes is his wife, sails from burning Troy for home, but is shipwrecked on the Egyptian coast. He leaves the phantom Helen in a cave and seeks help. He finds the real Helen, but refuses to believe in her until the phantom Helen flies off into the sky. He now has the problem of getting the real Helen away from the Egyptians.

The Pharaoh, desiring Helen, issues orders to kill all Greeks who might come seeking her, but Helen devises a trick. She sees the Egyptian king and claims a messenger has brought word that her husband Menelaus has been killed. She promises to marry the king if he will allow her to make proper burial honors to her dead husband. He agrees. Menelaus, who is disguised as the messenger who brought the sad news to Helen, then tells the Egyptian how Greek burial honors are conducted for a king who has drowned in the sea. A ship must be taken offshore. It must be loaded with sacrificial food, which the widow must personally throw into the sea.

The king gives the order. Menelaus manages to smuggle his shipwrecked sailors onto the boat. Once at sea they overpower the Egyptian guards and sail back to Sparta, where they live happily ever after.

Helen does not have so happy a time of it in an account retold by Pausanias. After Menelaus dies, she is driven from Sparta by the angry people. They resent her because of the number of Spartans killed at Troy, and also because she was the sister of the hateful Clytemnestra, who killed Agamemnon, Menelaus' brother. Helen flees to the island of Rhodes, but the queen of Rhodes, who lost her husband at Troy, takes vengeance on the hapless Helen by having her servants hang the fugitive.

The classical writers were not content just to tell what happened to the surviving heroes of the Trojan War. Beginning with Homer, they followed them into the ghost world. Earlier we mentioned how Odysseus goes to Hades on a visit and Achilles tells him that it is better to be a slave on earth than king of the dead. Odysseus also meets Agamemnon, who tells him how Clytemnestra caused his death.

In the second century A.D., Lucian of Samostrata pictured the Trojan heroes in the afterworld. He did this both in A *True Story* and in *The Dialogues of the Dead*. A *True Story* was the forerunner of *Gulliver's Travels, Baron Munchausen,* and other tall tales. While most writers go to extreme lengths to make their stories believable, Lucian, in the introduction to A *True Story*, warns the reader to believe nothing in it. For this reason alone, he probably comes closer to the truth than all the others.

In the course of a series of astounding adventures that poke fun at Homer, Herodotus, Pausanias, and others, Lucian and his crew finally come to the island where the shades of former men and women now reside. The ghosts are as quarrelsome as people, and the visitors find a number of lawsuits in progress. One is an argument between Theseus of Athens and Menelaus of Sparta over which one will live with Helen. Theseus had stolen her when she was still a child, and he considered himself her first husband. Naturally the first comes first. Rhadamanthus, as judge, awards Helen to Menelaus. His reasoning is that Menelaus went to considerable trouble and faced death in the Trojan War for her. Also Theseus has three wives already.

The heroes have a very nice place in which to spend their eternities. The houses are of gold built on streets of ivory. The outer wall is built of huge emeralds instead of rocks. A river of perfume circles the city. The heroes are actual spirits without flesh or bones, but one cannot tell that by looking at them. Their clothing is spun of fine cobwebs. They never age, but remain as they were when they arrived.

Everyone is there. Homer recites poems in the evening. Helen, of generous spirit, forgives all the writers for the bad things they have written about her. And the heroes quarrel as they did in life.

Lucian corners Homer and asks if he really did write the *Iliad* and the *Odyssey*. The argument over the authorship of these epics was alive even in the classical Greek period. Homer says his name, Homeros, means "hostage" and that he got it because he was taken from his native Babylon to Greece as a hostage. Homer stoutly insists that he wrote every line of the *Iliad* and the *Odyssey* and that those who claim the Catalogue of Ships and other parts were inserted by later editors are wrong. One of the characters in the *Iliad* sues him for libel, implying that all in the epic was not the complete truth. However, Homer retains Odysseus as his attorney and wins the case.

There is a battle when some convicts on an adjoining island escape, but the heroes under Theseus and Achilles defeat them. This inspires Homer to write a new epic, and he gives Lucian a copy to carry back from hell to the earth. Unfortunately it is lost later, depriving the world of an epic equal to or better than the *Iliad*. All Lucian can recall are its opening lines:

> Sing, heavenly muse, of Hell's first revolution
> When dead heroes fought for their blessed isle.

The Elysian Fields of the heroes is a very nice place indeed, and Lucian would be glad to stay, but unfortunately one of his ship-wrecked crew, a handsome young man, falls in love with Helen. Then, emulating Paris, he runs away with her. Naturally Menelaus, having had experience in this sort of thing, knows what to do. He calls his brother Agamemnon, who rouses the Greeks, and they set sail once more in pursuit.

The eloping pair are captured and brought back. Helen weeps with embarrassment, but Lucian and his mortal crew are banished back to earth.

While Lucian laughs at Helen in *A True Story*, he treats her memory more kindly in one of his *Dialogues of the Dead*. In this satire, Menippus, a Cynic, commits suicide. Having sought death, he does not—like his fellow passengers on Charon's boat across the Styx River to Hades—fear hell. He jokes and pokes fun at his fellow shades. Once across the river he asks the god Hermes to show him the beautiful women of bygone times, especially Helen of Troy.

Hermes points to a collection of bones, designating one skull as that of the famous Helen.

"This is what launched a thousand ships from every part of Greece?" Menippus asks in wonder, as he gazes on the skull.

Hermes replies, "Ah, Menippus, you never saw the youthful Helen. If you had, even a Cynic like you would have said that none could be blamed for suffering for the sake of one like her."

He compares human beauty to the flower that blossoms and then fades in ugliness. Menippus wants to know why the Greeks at Troy did not realize that they were fighting for something that was so short-lived. Hermes ignores his question, because the explanation for the actions of men where the beauty of a woman like Helen is concerned is a philosophic matter that the god does not have time to go into.

8

THE LAST TROYS

Schliemann sought Homer's Troy with a fanatic passion, and he found its site—none can deny him that honor. But he never knew the real Troy. In his hunger to get to the bedrock city and later to expose as much of Troy II as possible, he dug through and destroyed practically all that remained of the city he actually sought.

Although the little that remains bears out Homer and tradition that the Trojan War was fought somewhere around 1270–1260 B.C., the archaeological remains indicate that the Greeks were wrong in assuming that Troy was totally destroyed by Agamemnon's forces. Archaeology indicates that there was no break in culture between Troy VII-a, Homer's city, and Troy VII-b, the succeeding stratum. After the city was sacked and burned, the original inhabitants apparently came back within a comparatively short time. This may have been anywhere from a few days to a few years, but was not long enough for them to acquire a different way of doing things or a different way of life.

Blegen says that the returning Trojans rebuilt their homes on the shattered foundations of the previous city. The walls were restored, using the remaining portions of Troy VII-a, as that city had used what still stood after the disastrous earthquake that ended Troy

115

Heinrich Schliemann in middle age, from *Ilios, the City and Country of the Trojans,* 1880.

VI. Thus, when we view the extensive remains of Troy VI's walls, we are looking upon a portion of Homer's Troy and the succeeding Troy VII-b$_1$ and VII-b$_2$.

A new mystery appears in the Troy VII multistrata. The debris at the bottom of stratum VII-b shows that the people who returned to rebuild Homer's city were the same, or at least of the same culture, as those who occupied the doomed city. However, the upper levels show a distinct change. The upper levels of Troy VII-b revealed a new type of pottery, which was labeled knobbed ware by the excavators because of knobby projections molded in the clay.

This knobbed ware was more than just an introduction of a new design, which might happen because a potter showed a burst of artistic inspiration. The new pottery was all handmade. The potter's wheel, which had been in use for centuries, had suddenly disappeared. This level also disclosed hammers, axes, and other bronze

Handmade knobbed ware was left by the mysterious people who moved into Troy VII-b 2. Woodcut from Schliemann's *Ilios*.

implements. Both the tools and the knobby pottery bear a resemblance to similar artifacts found in Hungary along the Danube, and both have been dated to the Late Aegean Bronze Age. However, experts found sufficient differences in the material from the two locations to rule out the possibility that the new people came from Hungary. Heinrich Schmidt, a German archaeologist, suggested that these new Trojans may have come from Thrace. Without totally agreeing with Schmidt, Blegen felt that they had certainly come from across the Hellespont.

Ilhan Aksit feels that the newcomers may have been members of the Doric Greeks, who came from the north to destroy Mycenae soon after the fall of Troy. He points out that the great Hittite empire in Anatolia, Turkey, collapsed about 1180 B.C. "The new migrations, which we call Dorian raids, caused the collapse of the Hittites in Anatolia," he wrote. "A branch of these tribes coming from the Balkans appears at Troy. In the second phase of Troy VII-b, we see a new race, new traditions in this city. It is very probable that a part of these migrations invaded Troy and settled there."

Aksit dates the Homeric city from 1300 to 1200 B.C. Blegen gives it a shorter life, from 1300 to 1260. He dates VII-b_1 from 1260 to 1190 and the mysterious VII-b_2 from 1190 to 1100.

The end of the knobbed ware makers at Troy is as mysterious as their beginning. No evidence was found in the debris of VII-b_1 that they had to fight for their new home. Neither is there any sign of fire or earthquake to explain why the last of the original Trojans left or turned over the Hissarlik site to the knobbed ware people. Perhaps they moved into a deserted city. Perhaps the last of the Trojans fled at their approach. Not enough evidence exists even to draw a good theory.

The first Trojans came out of the mists of prehistory around 3000 B.C., lived at Hissarlik until about 1190 B.C. and then vanished as mysteriously as they had come. Their successors lived there ninety years by Blegen's chronology and three hundred years by Aksit's (from 1200 to 900 B.C.), and in the end they, too, vanished as completely as the original Trojans.

A lot of what happened might have been better revealed if Heinrich Schliemann had not destroyed so much of the upper strata in his obsession to reveal Troy II, which he mistakenly thought was the Homeric Troy. In the last year of his life Schliemann, impressed by Dörpfeld's arguments, also began to doubt his previous certainty about Troy II and made plans for extensive new diggings in Troy VI. He never lived to make them. As was his custom, he traveled during the off-season, when excavations at Troy had to stop. In the winter of 1890 he went alone to Italy after visiting Paris. He was in pain from an ear infection that had troubled him for years. However, he had heard that new material excavated from Pompeii was on exhibition at the museum in Naples, and he was eager to see it. Despite increasing illness he insisted on driving by carriage from Naples to Pompeii to see the ruins themselves. He returned to Naples and collapsed while walking on the street on Christmas Day.

He was rushed to a hospital, but his right side was paralyzed, and the ear infection had attacked his brain. The doctors could do nothing for him, and he died the day after Christmas. Dörpfeld and Sophia's brother came for the body and escorted it back to Athens, where it lay in state in the royal palace on January 4, 1891.

Messages of sympathy and respect poured in from all over the world. William Gladstone, former British Prime Minister and a deep student of Greek history, paid a tribute to the dead man:

> He had to encounter in the early stages of his work both frowns and indifference, yet the one and the other alike had to give way, as the force and value of his discoveries became clear, like mists before the sun. The history of his boyhood and youth were not less remarkable than that of his later life. Indeed, they cannot be separated, for one aim and purpose moved them from first to last.

Sophia Schliemann, immediately after her husband received a hero's funeral, announced that his work would continue. She made Dörpfeld a grant, and he returned to Hissarlik for another season's work. When this money ran out, Dörpfeld obtained financial assistance from the German government that made it possible to excavate until 1894. The excavations then ceased, although evaluations of the collections continued. Valuable work was done by Dörpfeld, but Schliemann had already done the spectacular work and uncovered the treasures.

Formal archaeological excavations were not resumed at Hissarlik until 1932, and they continued to 1938. This work was conducted by Carl Blegen in the field, but was due to the enthusiasm of Professor William T. Semple, who organized the Cincinnati Archaeological Expedition, as the group was called. The report of the expedition is contained in four large volumes published by the Princeton University Press.

Dörpfeld was the first to put the Trojan excavations on a scientific basis, but the Cincinnati Expedition was the first to employ modern archaeological techniques. Blegen was able to demonstrate, and Dörpfeld finally agreed, that the German archaeologist had been wrong in ascribing the Homeric city to Troy VI, and that the true city of Priam was stratum VII-a.

The Cincinnati Group made an exhaustive study of areas not covered by Schliemann and Dörpfeld and reevaluated the work of its predecessors. Some areas were not excavated because to do so would destroy valuable later sites. So, as far as anyone knows, there may still be treasures hidden in the Trojan levels. To get under the preserved remains would require tunneling and extremely expensive shoring and supporting. The price is more than anyone cares to pay for what they think the results will be.

In 1938 the Cincinnati Expedition considered the site worked out and moved to Mycenae. Nothing has been done at the site since then, although it is open to tourists.

Blegen's chronology ends with Troy VII-b$_2$ in 1100 B.C. and does not pick up Troy VIII until 900 B.C., leaving a gap of two hundred years or more in which the city was abandoned. Aksit does not believe there was a break. He thinks the Trojans living in the Plains of Troy gradually ousted or assimilated the unknown knobbed ware people who populated Troy VII-b$_2$.

It isn't possible to agree entirely with either theory. Troy seems definitely to have been abandoned for a time, but whether this was as long as Blegen theorizes is debatable. However, it was certainly long enough for the torrential winter rains of the Troad to decompose the sun-dried brick and cover the debris of the former Troy. Then the newcomers, who were definitely Greek this time, built Troy VIII above the former city.

The continuation of Troy without a long break fits in with Homer's statements that Aeneas was destined to rule over the Trojans, implying that they would continue. However, it does not tie in with the traditions that Aeneas wandered to Italy and—as related by Vergil in the *Aeneid*—founded the line that led through Romulus and Remus to the founding of Rome.

Troy VIII lasted 550 years, from 900 B.C. to 350 B.C. It was in its middle period when Homer, according to traditional dating, wrote the *Iliad*. Thus, for the last half of this Troy's existence, we have some written references to back up the archaeological evidence. Although many writers claim that no written material was found in the early Troys, they are not entirely correct. Seals and inscriptions have been found. A. H. Sayce made a detailed study of these without coming to a concrete conclusion. He says that the inscriptions found proved that writing was known in this region "long before the introduction of the Phoenician or Greek alphabet. Inscribed objects are not plentiful, but sufficient exist to show that the ancient inhabitants were not wholly illiterate." He attempts to show that the Trojan inscriptions are similar to markings found in Cyprus, which he dates at around 1800 B.C.

One inscription design is carved intaglio on a cylinder of feldspar. (Intaglio is a form of decoration in which the image is carved into the surface of the material and is depressed *below* it, in contrast to relief work, in which the image is raised *above* the surface.) This cylinder—but not the inscription—resembles those of Babylon. They were rolled on wet clay to impress their form there. If the Trojans did their writing on wet, unbaked clay, as this indicates, then it might account for the dearth of written material. The records,

Ruins of an altar from Troy VIII. In the foreground is a sacrificial place with a gutter for the blood to run through.

like the house bricks, would have melted in the centuries of rain. This also happened on Crete. The reason much written material was preserved on Crete is because the terrific fire that destroyed Knossos hardened many of the written records.

Still, if this theory is true, we would expect some records to have been similarly burned in the great fires of Troy II and Troy VII-a.

The builders of Troy VIII introduced something new. Instead of just filling in areas with debris to level the foundations of their new construction, as was previously the case, the new builders removed levels from the top of the highest point in the city in order to find a firm foundation for a temple they raised to Athena. In this area Schliemann found a giant *pithos*—jar— that was considerably taller than a man. It was made of red clay mixed with silicates and mica. "It was thoroughly baked," Schliemann wrote, "which, as Prince Bismarck [Germany's Iron Chancellor] suggested to me, could, in the absence of kilns, only have been effected by kindling a fire simultaneously both within and without it."

Schliemann did not make a careful examination of these top layers. His account of them is accurate in what he describes, but is erroneous and mixed up in chronology. He lumps the Hellenistic Troy VIII and the Roman Troy IX together in what he called the Seventh City.

Troy VIII is well noted in ancient histories. Herodotus tells how Xerxes, the Persian king, stopped at Troy on his way to fight the Greeks in 480 B.C. He sacrified a thousand bulls to the Ilian Athena in honor of the dead heroes. The *Iliad* was well known at the Persian court. Xerxes honored Trojans because they, like himself, were bitter enemies of the Greeks. After leaving Troy, Xerxes took his army to Abydos, just above the site of the present city of Canakkale, and had his engineers build a bridge of boats across the Hellespont over which he crossed to his ultimate defeat at the battle of Salamis.

Between the visit of Xerxes to Troy in 480 B.C. and its next great visitor, Alexander the Great, in 334 B.C., Troy had the doubtful honor of again being defeated by a horse.

The first horses that betrayed Troy were mythical. These were the immortal horses of Laomedon, which caused Heracles to sack the city in Priam's father's time. The second was the wooden horse of Homer. The third was a real horse for the first time.

The story is told both by Plutarch and Polyaenus, but with variations. The orator Demosthenes likewise made a reference to the story, but included no details.

It seems that a mercenary soldier named Charidemus fled to Asia Minor, where he apparently was able to mass a private army. About 356 B.C., Charidemus made arrangements with a Trojan slave to betray the city. The man had to have an excuse to get the Trojan gate open. So Charidemus

> gave him many sheep and slaves to bring in, twice or three
> times. The watchmen, having distributed these, permitted the
> slave to go out in the night along with men to help bring in the
> booty.
>
> Charidemus seized and bound those who had come with
> the slave, dressed his own men in their clothes, and gave them
> booty along with a horse as if it too had been captured. The
> watchmen, in order to receive the horse, opened the whole
> gate. Charidemus' soldiers then rushed in, killed the watch-
> men, and, having encountered the rest of the force, stormed
> the city. If we may make a jest, Ilion was taken for the second
> time by the stratagem of a horse.

Plutarch says that the horse fell (was killed?) in the gate, which
prevented the guard from closing it soon enough to prevent
Charidemus' men from rushing in.

Plutarch, in his life of Alexander, tells how the young conqueror stopped at Troy on his way to meet the Persian forces of
Darius II at the Granicus River in 334 B.C. He sacrificed to Athena at
the temple and to the ghosts of the Trojan heroes. He then went to
the tomb of Achilles between Troy and the sea. There he anointed
the funeral column with oil and ran naked around the tomb in a
customary tribute to the great warrior. This funeral column is not
mentioned in ancient accounts of Achilles' funeral.

Alexander also placed a wreath of flowers on the tomb and
praised Achilles for being a true friend because of his actions in
avenging the death of Patroclus.

Arrian adds that Alexander hung his own armor in the temple of
Athena and accepted some armor that had been preserved from the
Trojan War. He did not wear the ancient armor, but had it carried
into battle by his guards. Later he made sacrifices to the ghost of King
Priam, begging him to withhold his wrath, because Alexander was of
the blood of Neoptolemus, Achilles' son, who killed Priam at the
sack of Troy.

Concerning the appearance of Troy VIII at this time, Strabo wrote:

> It is said that the city of the present Ilians was until then a small market-town, and that it had a small and insignificant temple of Athena. But Alexander, having ascended to it after the battle of Granicus, adorned the temple with offerings, raised the town to the rank of a city, commanded the wardens to enlarge it by new buildings, and declared the city free and exempt from all taxes.

This was during Alexander's second visit to Troy. The first, when he made his naked run around Achilles' grave, occurred on his way to Granicus. He apparently attributed his success in the battle to Athena and to the ghosts of Troy, and showed his appreciation by these honors to the city. Strabo continues:

> At a later time, after the conquest of the Persian empire, Alexander sent to Ilium a very kind letter, promising to make it a large city, to make its temple celebrated, and to institute sacred games in the city. After Alexander's death, Lysimachus [Alexander's general] did much for the city, surrounded it with a wall, built a temple, and increased the population by adding to it the inhabitants of the old neighboring cities, which were in decay. He did this for Alexander who felt a great interest in Ilium, both on account of his relationship with the Ilians, and because of his admiration for Homer.
>
> There has been handed down a corrected edition of the Homeric poems, called "the edition of the casket," because Alexander revised and annotated these poems with the aid of the pupils of Callisthenes and Anaxarchus, and preserved them in a richly ornamented casket, which he had found in a Persian treasury.
>
> Alexander's great kindness toward the Ilians proceeded, therefore, in the first place from his veneration of the poet, and, secondly, from his relationship with the Aeacids, the kings of Molossians, among whom, as is said, Andromaché also reigned.

The tradition through all these years was that Troy continued to occupy the same location. However, New Ilium, as the Greek and Roman Troys were called, did not occupy the Hissarlik outcropping as the first seven Troys did. New Ilium was located on the plain behind Hissarlik. Nevertheless, New Ilium used the Hissarlik mound as its acropolis, and it was here that they maintained the temple of Athena and apparently a temple of Zeus, as well. During the Roman Troy IX period, there was also a small marble theater here, along with a Roman bath. Thus the old Troy served as a cultural center for the new Troy.

Although the last Troys lived during historical times and have much written documentation, their chronology is even more hazy than some of the early cities with their clearly defined strata. Aksit dates Troy VIII from 900 to 350 B.C. and Troy IX from 350 B.C. to A.D. 400. All dates are admittedly guesses, of course. If we restrict Troy VIII to the Hellenic period and make Troy IX entirely Roman, then this chronology dating is too short for Troy VIII. Lysimachus rebuilt the temple of Athena and enlarged the city after Alexander's death in 323 B.C.

We might be on much safer ground historically if we date the end of Troy VIII to sometime between 250 and 200 B.C. We pick this date because Antiochus the Great (242–187 B.C.), the king of Syria who expanded his empire into southern Turkey, was in control of this area until the Romans expelled his troops in 190–189 B.C.

Demetrius of Scepsis visited New Ilium at this time and reported that the houses were very much in decay. He implies that the place had no walls, although Polybius states definitely that the city had fortified walls in 218 B.C., which was twenty-one years before Demetrius' visit. This proves only that New Ilium was definitely occupied to the time of the Roman invasion, although by a poverty-stricken people. The acropolis on Hissarlik had not lost its reputation, however, for Livy tells how Antiochus the Great came by sea to New Ilium in 190 B.C. to sacrifice at the Athena temple before his expulsion by the Roman victory.

Justin reports that the first Romans to land in Asia were wel-

Roman theater from Troy IX, circa A.D. 400.

comed with joy by the Ilians. The Romans reciprocated, and the meeting was "as if parents and children met after a long separation."

The Romans, because they considered Aeneas their ancestor, took a tremendous interest in the city. Schliemann wrote in his book *Ilios, the City and Country of the Trojans:*

The Romans, who were proud of their origin from Ilium and Aeneas, treated the city of their heroic ancestors with signal munificence, adding to its domain the adjacent territories of Sigeum, Rhoeteum, and Gergis, as well as the whole coast from the Peraea [or continental territory] of Tenedos [this is the coastal area of the Troad opposite the island of Tenedos], southward of Sigeum, to the confines of Dardanus. The Sigeans would not submit to this loss of autonomy, and their city was therefore destroyed by the Ilians.

Grote, whose *History of Greece* was the standard work during the late nineteenth century, observed that because of this Roman interest in New Ilium, "we must find it but natural that the Ilians assumed to themselves exaggerated importance, as the recognized parents of all-conquering Rome. Partly, as we may naturally suppose, from the jealousies thus aroused on the part of their neighbors . . . and partly from the tendency of the age . . . toward criticism and illustration of the old poets, a blow was now aimed at the legitimacy of Ilium."

Schliemann writes that the leaders in this new Trojan war—

the attempt to destroy the traditional glory of Ilium—were, first, Demetrius of Scepsis, a most laborious Homeric critic . . . who was ambitious of proving that his native city, Scepsis, had also been the royal residence of Aeneas; and secondly, Hestiaea, an authoress of Alexandria-Troas, who had also written comments on the *Iliad*, and had made researches as to whether the Trojan war could have taken place before New Ilium.

This was the beginning of two thousand years of argument about the location of Homer's Troy, which was not entirely settled until 1938, when Blegen convinced everyone that Troy VII-a was the "real" Troy. The argument was very much alive when Schliemann put forth his claims for Troy II in 1871, and it took him nineteen more years to get archaeologists and historians even to admit that he might have found the site of the place.

New Ilium had a hectic history in the Roman period. In 85 B.C. the city was attacked by a Roman rebel during Rome's war with

Mithridates VI (132–63 B.C.), king of Pontus, an ancient kingdom on the Black Sea. According to Strabo, the war with Mithridates was being directed by Valerius Flaccus, who was murdered by his second-in-command, Fimbria. Strabo writes:

> Fimbria made himself commander-in-chief of the army and marched against Ilium. When the Ilians refused to receive him as being a brigand, he attacked the city by force and took it in ten days. When he glorified himself upon having overpowered in ten days the city which Agamemnon, with his fleet of a thousand ships and the whole power of Hellas, had hardly been able to conquer in the tenth year, one of the Ilians said, "It happened because we had no Hector to fight for the city."
>
> Fimbria was soon attacked and destroyed by Sulla (138–78 B.C.), the Roman general and dictator . . . who consoled the Ilians by making many improvements in their city. In our time the divine Caesar did yet more for Ilium. . . ."

Appian, who wrote two hundred years after Strabo, had a somewhat different version of Fimbria's attack on Ilium. He probably used his imagination, or else Strabo's story had grown with two hundred years of retelling. Appian implies that the Ilians may have been collaborating with Mithridates. He writes:

> The Ilians, being besieged by Fimbria, applied to Sulla, who told them he would come. He ordered them to tell Fimbria that they had given themselves up to Sulla. Whe Fimbria heard this, he praised them as being already friends of the Romans, requested them to receive him as he was also a Roman, and ironically referred to the affinity existing between Romans and Ilians.
>
> But when he entered the city, he murdered all who came in his way, burned the whole city, and in various ways shamefully treated those who had gone as ambassadors to Sulla. He neither spared the sanctuaries nor those who had fled to the temple of Athena, for he burned them together with the temple.
>
> He also pulled down the walls, and went round on the

following day, to see whether anything of the town still remained standing. The town suffered more than under Agamemnon, and perished root and branch by the hand of a kinsman; not a house of it was saved, nor a temple nor an idol. But the statue of Athena, called the Palladium, which is held to have fallen from heaven, some believe was found unhurt.

Whatever may be the truth in Appian's account of the sack of the city, his statement about the Palladium is certainly at odds with the classical Greek writers. It is a foundation of the Trojan legend that the Palladium was given to the city when it was founded and that Troy would never fall as long as it remained in the city. Therefore, the Palladium had to be stolen. This was accomplished by Diomedes and Odysseus, who stole into the city at night. It was one of the celebrated exploits of the Trojan war.

Lucan in his *Pharsalia* tells how Julius Caesar visited the site of Troy, and Seutonius, in his life of Caesar, tells how the Roman dictator, who traced his ancestry back to Aeneas, planned to make Troy the capital of the Roman empire.

9

TROY IN THE CHRISTIAN ERA

Augustus, grandnephew of Julius Caesar and the first emperor of Rome, ruled from 27 B.C. to A.D. 14. He also was an admirer of Ilium, and Horace, the Roman poet, attributed to him a plan similar to Caesar's in which Rome would have its capital at Troy.

In an ode Horace has the Roman goddess Juno (the Greek Hera) promising that the Romans will reign as long as the wide sea separates Troy and Rome and that Rome will stand as long as herds trample over the tumulus of Priam. This ode has been used by many through the years as proof that Troy, or Ilium, was not rebuilt by the Romans.

Schliemann quotes Eckenbrecher:

We must explain Horace only to have intended to rebuke the *exaggerated piety* displayed in the restoration of Troy, and *not* its restoration generally. Seutonius perhaps gives us an explanation of the poet's motives for saying this in such emphatic words. He tells us, in fact, that shortly before Caesar's assassination there had been a strong and universally diffused rumor that Caesar intended to transfer the center of gravity of Roman power to Ilium. . . . Such plans may also have hovered in the air at the time of Augustus, and may have induced Horace,

131

who held them to be pernicious, to express himself in the sharpest manner.

If Augustus really admired Ilium so much, it did not prevent him from severely punishing the city. Schliemann quotes Eduard Meyer, who in turn quotes Nicolaus of Damascus, that "Julia, daughter of Augustus, unexpectedly came by night to Ilium. In passing the Scamander, which had overflowed and was very swift, she had a narrow escape of being drowned. Julia's husband, Agrippa, punished the Ilians by imposing a fine of a hundred thousand denarii, for not having made provision for the safety of the princess; but they had not been able to do so, as they were totally ignorant of Julia's intention to visit their city."

Augustus did not object to the punishment, but later ordered its remission.

An inscription found in New Ilium indicates that Caius Caesar, Julia's son and the adopted son of his grandfather, Augustus, visited Ilium. The inscription calls the young man, who was made governor of Roman Asia at nineteen, the kinsman, benefactor, and patron of the city.

In succeeding years both Nero and Claudius took an interest in New Ilium. In A.D. 53, before he was emperor, Nero made a speech to the Forum in Rome in which he lauded the Ilians. Claudius, according to Seutonius, freed the Ilians of all public taxes.

The next emperor of Rome who admired the Trojans was Caracalla, who reigned from A.D. 211 to 217. No man, not even Schliemann, carried his admiration to greater lengths than this peculiar Roman.

Quoting Herodian:

Caracalla first visited all the remains of Ilium and was shown the relics of ancient Troy. He then went to the tomb of Achilles, and having adorned it sumptuously with wreaths and flowers, he again imitated Achilles. Being in want of a Patroclus, he did as follows: one of his freedmen, Festus by name, was his most intimate friend, and keeper of the imperial archives. This Festus died when Caracalla was at Ilium. Some people said he was poisoned in order that he might be buried like Patroclus, but others said he died from illness.

Caracalla ordered the funeral, and that a great pile of wood should be heaped up for the pyre. Having the body in the midst, and having slaughtered all kinds of animals, the emperor kindled the fire, and taking a cup he made libations to the winds and prayed. As he was very bald-headed and tried to put a lock of his hair in the fire, he was laughed at, for he cut off all the hair he had.

Schliemann believed that the resulting tumulus heaped over the bones is that now called Ujek Tepe, the largest of the heroic tumuli in the Troad.

The rise of Christianity in the third and fourth centuries had a definite effect upon the future of Troy. The Christians naturally were against the pagan gods with whom Troy and Ilium were associated. They smashed many temples in their religious zeal, but Constantine the Great, the first Christian Roman emperor (he reigned A.D. 306–337), kept the Roman regard for Troy.

Wrote Schliemann:

When Constantine the Great decided upon building a new capital for his vast empire, which was definitely to replace ancient Rome, he intended at first to found Nova Roma in the land of the ancient ancestors of the Romans. According to Zosimus, he chose a site between Alexandria-Troas and the ancient Ilium; according to Zonaras, he chose a site on Sigeum. There Constantine laid the foundations of the city. Part of the wall had already been built when he gave the preference to the much more suitable Byzantium.

Byzantium became Constantinople, capital of the Byzantine Empire, and today's Istanbul.

Emperor Julian, who had a short reign from 361 to 363, made a trip to New Ilium about A.D. 354 before he became emperor. Carl Henning found a letter Julian wrote about the visit. It is in the British

Museum. Julian had gone to Ilium to investigate secretly reports about one Pegasius who tended the ancient temples.

Schliemann reports the letter in full:

> We should never easily have had anything to do with Pegasius, had we not been convinced that formerly, whilst he appeared to be a bishop of the Galileans, he knew how to respect and honor the gods. . . . A great many rumors were current about him and came to my ears, and by the gods, I thought that he deserved to be hated more than the most depraved wretches. But when . . . I reached Ilium at the time of full market (between nine and ten in the morning), he came to meet me and became my guide, as for one who wished to know the city (this being my pretext for visiting the temples). He led me about everywhere to show me the curiosities.
>
> Listen then, to facts and words from which one may suppose him to be not regardless of the gods. There is a sanctuary of Hector, where a bronze statue stands in a small chapel. Opposite to him they have put up Achilles in the open air. . . . Happening to find the altars still burning, and I might say almost still in a blaze, and Hector's statue anointed with fat, I looked at Pegasius and said, "What is the meaning of these sacrifices to the Ilians?"—sounding him in a delicate way in order to learn how his feelings were.
>
> He answered: "What is there unbecoming if they do homage to a good man, their citizen, just as we do to the martyrs?"
>
> What then happened afterwards? "Let us go," I said, "into the sacred precepts of the Ilian Athena." He also most willingly led the way, opened to me the temple, and, as if calling me to witness, he showed me the statues perfectly well preserved. He did none of the things those impious men are wont to do, who make on the forehead the sign of the impious [that is, the sign of the cross], nor did he hiss to himself. . . .
>
> The same Pegasius followed me also to the Achilleum, and showed me the sepulchre unhurt, for I had heard also that he had excavated this tomb. But he approached it even with great reverence.

Coins found in New Ilium show, left, Hector slaying Patroclus, and, right, the fight for Patroclus' body.

All this I saw myself. But I have heard from those who are now inimically disposed against him, that in secret he prays to and worships the sun. Would you not accept my testimony, even as a private man? Of the sentiments which each one of us has regarding the gods, who could be more credible witnesses than the gods themselves? . . . Should we not be ashamed to treat him just as Aphobius did and as all the Galileans pray to see him treated?

If you listen at all to me, you will honor not him alone, but also the others who go over [from Christianity to heathenism], in order that these may follow us easily when we summon them to the good way, and that the others [the Christians] may rejoice the less. But if we drive away those who come of themselves, nobody will readily follow when we invite them.

Apparently, even at the time he wrote this enlightening letter, Julian—called Julian the Apostate by the Christians—was already plotting a return to heathenism. In commenting on the letter, Schliemann pointed out that it proved that New Ilium was still in existence and that the temples were still open on the Hissarlik mound in A.D. 354. In a footnote to the letter, Schliemann wrote:

> In spite of all edicts against the worship of ancient gods, Troy must still have been under the first Christian emperors a place of pilgrimage for the heathen world. The city, with all its temples, was indeed more than neglected by the emperors; but nevertheless we find it treated better than other cities, if we remember that by the edict of 324 A.D., repeated in 341, the service of the Hellenic worship of gods was prohibited in the East. The temples themselves were confiscated in 326, and many of them were destroyed, partly by order of the authorities, partly with their express or tacit consent.

This letter is the last written evidence of the city's existence. However, Roman coins of a later date were found in the ruins, so that the A.D. 400 date for the end of Troy IX is not unreasonable. While nothing is known of its fall, the religious situation provides sufficient reason for thinking it was abandoned because of its association with the discredited Greek gods.

Unfortunately, none of the excavators showed too much interest in these last two Troys. They did not consider them as historically important as the earlier cities had been. Also, they were badly broken up by Schliemann's haste to expose the more important layers beneath them. Aksit and others have been extremely critical of Schliemann for this. However, Schliemann's own account indicates that he may not have been as destructive as his critics claim. Of the temple of Athena he was accused of destroying, he says:

> Little had escaped the pious zeal of the early Christians. The drums [that is, sections] of its Corinthian columns, with their beautiful capitals, all of white marble, had been used to build a wall of defense, the drums being joined with cement. In my trench on the southeast side I have been obliged to break

through this wall. The drums which I took out may be seen standing upright at the entrance of the trench. [Visitors to Troy today can still see them lying on the ground near the entrance to the ruins.] The floor of the temple consisted of slabs of limestone which rested upon double layers of the same stone. This was covered to a depth of 1 to 3 feet of vegetable matter. This explains the total absence of entire sculptures. Whatever sculptures remained were destroyed by fanaticism or wantonness. Judging from the foundations, the temple was 288 feet long by 72½ feet wide.

This temple was at Hissarlik, the site of ancient Troy, which the city of New Ilium used as an acropolis. The city itself was on the plain and was much larger than it had ever been in heroic times. Schliemann did some excavating, sinking shafts mainly to determine if additional layers existed there as they did on Hissarlik. When he found that there were none, he turned back to Hissarlik. Of New Ilium, the city, he says:

The vast extent of the city; the masses of marble or granite columns which peep out from the ground; the millions of fragments of sculptures with which the site is strewn; the many large heaps of ruins; the mosaic floors brought to light in various places; the gigantic aqueduct which still spans the river, and by which Ilium was provided with water from the upper part of the river; and last, not least, the vast theater, capable of seating 5,000 spectators, cut in the slope to the east of Hissarlik; all this testifies to the large size, the wealth, and the magnificence of the town.

After the abandonment of Troy in A.D. 400, soil from erosion, the debris from crumbling clay bricks, and growing vegetation covered the site. The magic of the *Iliad* and the *Odyssey* kept the name of Troy alive, but the site itself was forgotten. The collapse of the Byzantine Empire and the capture of Asia Minor by the Turks closed this area to Western people. Even the coming of the Renaissance, with its revival of concern with the ancient world, brought no interest in finding Troy. Not until the sixteenth century did travelers begin to show curiosity about the location.

In 1627 a man named Sandys published in London a book called A *Description of the Turkish Empire*. He told of landing on the shore of the Troad, but said he was prevented from going inland to seek the site of Troy because of bandits in the area. He was the first to write about the Ilium location since an Italian, Pietro Beloni, published a travel book in 1588.

Pococke, an Englishman, visited the Troad in 1739. He was the first known person to make a thorough study of the region in search of Troy or other remains of the Homeric period.

Then, about 1750, Lady Mary Wortley Montague, an Englishwoman who anticipated Heinrich Schliemann, took a voyage through the Hellespont from Constantinople and stopped at Cape Sigeum at the opening of the strait. She went inland with a copy of the *Iliad* as her guide, just as Schliemann was to do over a hundred years later, but she was unable to determine the site of Troy itself. She did, however, identify what she thought were the tumuli of Ajax and Achilles. She also identified the Simois River.

During this period, the general consensus placed the Troy site at Alexander-Troas on the coast of Besika Bay. (Today this is believed to be the spot where the Greek ships were beached during the battles.) This opinion changed in the late-eighteenth century after the investigations in 1786 of Le Chevalier, a French traveler and archaeologist, who wrote a short discourse on the subject, which he expanded, in 1802, into a three-volume account called *Voyage de la Troade*.

Le Chevalier was almost as enthusiastic an admirer of Homer as Schliemann later became. However, archaeology was then in its infancy, and Le Chevalier depended more upon "divine inspiration," spurred by Homer's writings, than by digging in the ground. After viewing the ruins at Bunarbashi on the hill Batieia in the foothills of Mount Ida, his divine inspiration assured him that this was sacred Ilium itself. Like Schliemann at a later date, Le

The partly excavated mound at Hissarlik as it appeared in 1879, as seen from the Simois River. Woodcut from Schliemann's *Ilios*.

Chevalier depended upon Homer's geographical descriptions to verify his theory. Homer mentioned hot and cold springs near the city, and when he found a hot spring along with several cold ones, he was assured that he was correct in calling this the site of Priam's city.

Le Chevalier's claims in his first treatise on Troy created a sensation among Homer lovers, but were not universally accepted. An Englishman, Jacob Bryant, wrote an angry denial in a book published by Eton College in 1796. It had the title, *Observations upon a Treatise entitled a 'Description of the Plain of Troy,' by M. Lechevalier.* Bryant believed that the story told in the *Iliad* was entirely a myth and that there never had been a Trojan War. He did agree that Homer had used actual sites he had seen himself to add realism to history, but he felt the locale was not in the so-called Plain of Troy.

And so the battle continued to rage down through the years. Schliemann listed a bibliography of over sixty books that made reference to the controversy. By the time he began his first excavations, critical opinion was generally on the side that thought the Trojan War to be a myth. Those who did believe in a real war leaned for the most part to Bunarbashi as the site of Ilium.

Schliemann's excavations proved them wrong. However, in light of claims that Dardanus had his original settlement in this area and that the settlers of Troy came from Dardanus, it appeared that Bunarbashi would be a fertile place to excavate, for the ruins should have been older than Troy VI.

Such did not prove to be the case. If the original Trojans settled first in the foothills of Mount Ida before the family split, with one branch going to Troy, then it was a different spot from Bunarbashi. In May, 1864, the Austrian consul-general to Turkey, J. G. von Hahn, and the famous astronomer, Julius Schmidt, dug at Bunarbashi. Hahn reported, "I can only confirm that the whole locality does not show the slightest trace of a great city ever having existed here, which ought to have extended over the wide northern slope of the Bali Dagh, from the foot of the Acropolis to the springs of Bunarbashi."

Schliemann, who dug at Bunarbashi before going to Hissarlik, got the same results. He reported:

My thorough exploration of the heights of Bunarbashi in August 1868 gave the same results. I excavated in hundreds of places at the springs, in Bunarbashi itself, and on the land between that village and the Scamander River, as well as on the declivities wherever I found earth. I struck the rock almost everywhere at a depth of from 2 to 3 feet, without ever finding the slightest vestige of bricks and pottery.

With regard to the walls brought to light by J. G. von Hahn and Julius Schmidt in the little city at the extremity of the Bali Dagh, in which so many great luminaries of archeology have seen the cyclopean walls of Priam's Pergamus . . . nearly all these walls are low retaining walls, formed of comparatively small quadrangular slabs. . . . There is also a fragment of wall of square hewn blocks in the south-west corner; but we have no right whatever to call these walls, or any part of them, "cyclopean."

As to the chronology of the little city on the Bali Dagh, we have fortunately two data for its determination: first by the manner in which the stones have been worked; and, secondly, from the pottery. On all the stones of the walls without exception, the blows of the stonecutters' iron pick-axes are conspicuous. Therefore, in my opinion, no part of them can claim a higher antiquity than the fourth or fifth century B.C.

The use of iron implements definitely shows that the Bunarbashi ruins do not belong to the Bronze Age. Rudolf Virchow, the great German pathologist and archaeologist, dated them no earlier than the time of Alexander the Great. This would make Bunarbashi contemporary with the Hellenistic Troy VIII. If there ever was a city of the original Trojans in the Mount Ida area, then it is still to be discovered.

10

THE TUMULI OF TROY

Scattered through the Troad are a number of tumuli, ancient burial mounds. At least Western investigators call such a mound a tumulus. The Turks refer to it simply as "tepe," which means a small hill. Tradition has assigned the names of various heroes to these tumuli, which naturally has attracted the attention of excavators hopeful of finding the usual treasure buried with a great hero. The fact that Xerxes, Alexander, and other notable visitors to the Troad supposedly stood over the grave sites of Achilles and Hector gives credence to traditions that these artificial mounds might well be heroic graves.

Schliemann quotes from the *Odyssey* concerning the funeral of Elpenor, a companion of Odysseus who died on Circe's island, to prove that the Achaeans of the Trojan war period did build up the tumulus over their dead: "We at once cut trunks of trees, and, sore grieved, performed his funeral on the high projecting shore, shedding abundant tears. And when the body was burnt with his weapons, we heaped up a tomb, erected a pillar on it, and put up on its highest point a well-fitting oar."

One of the most famous of the tumuli is the so-called tomb of Ajax at Intepe. This was originally right on the shore at the mouth of the Hellespont. Pausanias and Philostratus both claimed that the sea washed away part of the mound, exposing the body of Ajax. Philostratus said that the bones showed that the man had been eleven cubits tall. A cubit was a measurement from the elbow to the end of the middle finger. Allowing for the difference in human arms, this comes out to between eighteen and twenty-two inches. It would have made Ajax at the shortest sixteen and one half feet tall—truly the giant he was supposed to have been!

Hadrian, Roman emperor from A.D. 117 to 138, was said to have kissed the bones and ordered them reinterred in the present tumulus farther back from the sea, and to have erected a temple to the hero. The temple was destroyed and a famous statue of Ajax removed by Christian zealots. Later, in 1770, other stones were removed by a Turkish officer to get material for a bridge.

There is a small mount near the sea, which is believed to have been the original tumulus of Ajax. It stands on ground ten feet above the sea and is itself only three feet four inches high. In stormy weather the seas still rise over it. Schliemann sank a shaft into the remains but found nothing but pebbles.

Another famous tumulus is that of Achilles. It was opened with a shaft in 1786 by a crew working for the French ambassador to Istanbul. The tumulus was cone shaped. The top six feet consisted of hard-packed clay. After that came a compact layer of clay and stones two feet in depth. This was followed by first a layer of sand and clay and then a layer of fine sand. In the very center the excavator found a small stone cavity four feet square, which was covered by a flat stone. This covering stone had been broken by the mass of dirt above it.

Inside the cavity the excavator found charcoal, ashes mixed with fat, fragments of pottery, some human bones, an iron sword, and the small bronze figure of a man in a chariot. This list of articles was reported by Grafen Choiseul-Gouffier, for whom the excavation was made. Schliemann said doubtfully, "As no man of experience or worthy of confidence was present at the excavation, scholars seem to have distrusted the account from the first." Schliemann expressed the opinion that the excavator obtained the relics earlier and "found" them in order to please the ambassador. Schliemann based his opinion on the fact that nothing like this was found in any of the other tumuli. The iron sword definitely proved that the tomb was not that of Achilles, who lived in the Bronze Age.

Sophia Schliemann directed the excavation of the pasha tumulus, sinking a shaft down the center from the top. This mound is only a thousand yards from the New Ilium site and fits the description of Aesyetes' tomb. Priam's son Polites supposedly used its top as a watchtower to observe Greek maneuvers.

Schliemann, Homer in hand again, disagreed with Strabo's claim that the mound was Aesyetes' tomb. He considered it the tomb of Myriné, one of the Amazons. Local tradition assigned it to Batieia, the daughter of Teucer, who married Dardanus. Schliemann quotes A. H. Sayce to the effect that Myriné is identified with the Asiatic goddess Artemis–Cybele and that the Amazons were originally priestesses of this goddess of the hunt.

The original mound was heaped up on a rocky projection, and the tumulus itself stood thirty feet high, although its position on the rising ground made it appear higher. Mrs. Schliemann sank a shaft 10¾ feet long by 17½ feet wide through the center of the tumulus. She first encountered earth packed rock hard. Next there was heavy clay mixed with calcium and lime. Below this, at fifteen feet, she hit bedrock. The results were very disappointing to the excavators.

Schliemann reported:

> No ashes or charcoal were found. If a funeral pyre really existed, it is inconceivable that Mrs. Schliemann could have missed it when we consider the size of the cutting. There were found in the brown earth some fragments of hand-made pottery similar to that of the third, the burnt city of Hissarlik. [This is actually the second Troy, for the chronology of the layers had not been accurately determined when Schliemann wrote this in 1880.]

Later they found other pottery fragments that made Schliemann revise his idea that the tumulus was contemporary with Troy II.

However, he adds, "I find in the pottery no obstacle to my theory that the tumulus existed in the time of Homer [circa 750 B.C.]."

Schliemann next excavated the Ujek Tepe tumulus. *Ujek* in Turkish means "fireside." It is one of the largest in the Troad, measuring 213 feet in height. The name "fireside" came because for centuries bonfires were lighted on its summit by Christians who celebrated a festival there each August 1 in honor of Saint Elias. Schliemann thought they had confused the names Ilios and Elias and believed the tumulus was the sepulcher of the prophet.

Schliemann sank a ten-foot square shaft from the summit. He reported:

> I began my excavations by digging the first two days with picks and shovels only. The dirt was thrown out on the mound. The next two days I had to employ baskets to carry the dirt out. When the depth of the shaft reached 13 feet, I erected a wooden triangle—called by builders shear-legs—by means of which the earth was drawn out in baskets with windlasses.
>
> I struck at a depth of 2 feet, 8 inches below the summit, a wall which consisted alternately of roughly-hewn stones cemented with a quality of clay. The direction of the wall is from north to south. Having dug through the layers of ashes, I struck alternately layers of coarse yellow, brown, or whitish clay, which are intersected at intervals of from 4 to 5 feet by horizontal strata of unwrought stones. These could not, in my opinion, have been put there for any other purpose than to consolidate the tumulus.

As the shaft was deepened, Schliemann had to reduce its size. Loose dirt required shoring up the sides with large beams and planking. The digging became so dangerous that Schliemann was obliged to pay about $1.25 a day for each laborer. While work progressed on this shaft from the top, he started another that ran horizontally into the base of the tumulus. He discovered then that all the tumulus was not artificial; it had been built over a small hill.

The horizontal tunnel was dug through exceptionally hard ground and did not have to be supported by timbering, as the central

Ujek Tepe with the opening of Schliemann's horizontal shaft on the side and the wooden tower used to support his windlass at the top. Woodcut from *Ilois*.

shaft was. However, the tunnel was so narrow and hot and so fouled by the fumes of the kerosine lamps they needed to work by that the men could only stay there for short periods of time. When the tunnel finally connected with the shaft from the top, they celebrated with thirteen *okes* (thirty-two and one half bottles) of wine and two roast sheep, which Schliemann provided.

The workmen then dug galleries out from the horizontal shaft, discovering a covered tower. It was fifteen feet square at the base and rose thirty-nine feet four inches. Schliemann wrote:

I further ascertained that this tower had been founded directly above a circular enclosure, 4 foot, 4 inches high, consisting of well-cut polygons of rock which were so well fitted together that the whole enclosure appears to consist of one single block; its diameter being 34 feet. . . . Having cut a gallery into the massive square structure, I found in its midst, and 6 feet above its base, a quadrangular cavity 3 feet square and 5 feet high. It was filled with fine sand, which must in the course of ages have penetrated through the fissures between the stones. From this cavity I cut a vertical shaft through the masonry down to the virgin soil, without finding anything except some fragments of pottery. Among these, late Roman potsherds are conspicuous, and also there was an iron knife.

It was Schliemann's opinion that the structure upon which the tower was built had been some kind of a sacred shrine and was much older than the tower and the tumulus that covered them both. Schliemann seemed to think that the tower was constructed to give support to the tumulus itself.

This does not sound reasonable. Nothing that elaborate should have been necessary for this purpose. It could have been given additional support simply by piling up rock. The fact that the tower was built upon the foundation of a remarkably well-made altar of a much earlier period suggests a definite religious purpose. The entire system of structures was covered with dirt, clay, and debris, which suggests that they were either hidden deliberately from sight or were covered for protection to preserve them for a later day. Professor A. H. Sayce, of Oxford University, told Schliemann that he placed the altar at about the fifth century B.C. This would be contemporary with Troy VIII.

However, Schliemann, after careful study of historical records, believed that this was the tumulus Herodian claimed the mad emperor Caracalla (A.D. 211–216) erected for his friend Festus, whom he buried in the style of Patroclus.

The original tumulus of Patroclus was supposed to have been merely a cenotaph (that is, a memorial to someone buried elsewhere), which was enlarged later to include the bones of Achilles so that it then became the mound attributed to the latter. Since Caracalla tried to emulate Patroclus' funeral as set forth by Homer in the *Iliad*, Schliemann believed the tower—erected on the foundation of an earlier altar—was a cenotaph to Festus. Schliemann wrote:

> The identity of this tumulus with that of Festus is confirmed by its gigantic proportions. A vain fool like Caracalla, who aped the manners of Alexander the Great, and in cold blood murdered his dearest friend in order to imitate Achilles, could not but erect a funeral mound far exceeding in magnitude all the other tumuli of the Troad.

From an archaeological viewpoint the most interesting of all the tumuli investigated by Schliemann and others in the Troad was the Besika Tepe. This tumulus, which was not mentioned by ancient writers, is forty-eight feet three inches in height. The diameter is 266 feet at the base. Because of the ground elevation on which it was built, the tumulus is 141 feet above sea level at Besika Bay. The depression from which the dirt was taken to build the tumulus is nearby.

After sinking the usual shaft from the top, Schliemann had tunnels dug out from the central shaft, and the ground was much looser than in most of the other tumuli. The tunnels disclosed pottery of a completely different type from that he had encountered before. Later he compared these potsherds with all types of prehistoric pottery preserved in the British Museum, without finding anything to help him identify it.

There were two types, all of them hand-made. From the pieces found, the coarser examples appeared to have come from pots as large as three feet high. Schliemann reported:

> They are sometimes ornamented with a projecting rope-like band round the neck and a handle in the form of a rope. In general these coarse vessels are baked only to about one-third of the thickness of their clay. They far exceed in rudeness any pottery ever found by me in any one of the pre-historic cities of Hissarlik.

The smaller examples of the tumulus pottery were better made. Schliemann compared them to potsherds he had found in the lowest levels of Troy, but said that close examination proved them to be much different. They were made of a coarser clay to which more mica had been added, and they had only been baked from one third to one half their thickness, then polished both outside and inside.

The bottoms of the vases were flat, and many had been impressed by wickerwork so that the marks of the individual straws were plainly visible. Originally Schliemann thought that the marks had been caused by setting the clay on a wicker mat while the vases were being made, but they were so well done that they gave the impression of a deliberate attempt to create a pattern.

Schliemann, usually so ready to voice an opinion, hesitated to assign a definite date to the Besika Tepe pottery. He does state that the finds "most decidedly denote an altogether different race of people." Who were they? This is another of the many mysteries of Troy.

Others also delved into the mysteries of the tumuli. Frank Calvert, who owned part of Hissarlik mound, excavated in the so-called tumulus of Priam near Bali Dagh, the reputed site of Dardanus. The mound was very close to the small town that Schliemann had dug in without notable results. The tumulus was thirteen feet high, and part of a wall protruded from its side. Inside Calvert found a rock structure, square in form, made of large, roughly hewn stones. The open interior of the square was filled with small loose stones.

Calvert said that the structure appeared to be the base for some statue or public monument, but he quoted another investigator as being of the opinion that the structure was the foundation for an altar. There was no evidence that any body or bones had been buried there.

That is the curious thing about the so-called tumuli. Although the name "tumulus" means a burial place of a certain type, none of these mounds, except one, showed evidence of being used as such, and even that exception was reported upon doubtful authority. Many of them appeared to have altars hidden in their depths, but there is no real reason why an altar should have been covered with such a large mound.

Another point is that internal evidence apparently shows that construction of the tumuli was carried out over a long period of time. The Besika mound appears to be of a period around 2000 B.C., but some of the others are definitely identified with Troy VIII or possibly Troy IX.

Why were they built? What is their real significance? All we can say is that they resemble real tumuli found in other parts of Asia and Greece.

11

TROY IN WORDS

In the years that followed the end of Troy IX, the location may have been forgotten, but Troy remained alive in the written literature of the ages. Writers continued to give their own versions of the war, basing their stories upon Homer and Vergil for the most part, but enlivening them with ideas from their own imagination. One noticeable effect as time passed was the elimination of the gods and superstitious elements. Many, like Saint Augustine in *The City of God*, used Trojan elements to make relgous or moral points. Saint Augustine wrote to refute arguments that the fall of Rome to the Visigoths in A.D. 410 was due to the city's embracing Christianity and rejecting the old gods. Augustine pointed out that worship of the Greek gods had not kept Troy from being sacked—in fact, the jealous gods themselves had brought about the city's downfall.

Dictys' *Diary of the Trojan War* has been attributed to the fourth century A.D. However, the work has been called a literary forgery because it purports to be the actual diary of a man who fought in the Trojan war. This is a harsh condemnation, for writers had been using the "I was there" style long before Dictys—they still do—in order to add realism to their fiction. The introduction tells how the manuscript, written by a Greek soldier or a Cretan who fought on the side of the Greeks, was found in a tomb on Crete. The author tells much more than he claimed to have seen personally, quoting Odysseus as his authority for the events before the war and Neoptolemus, Achilles' son, for what came after. For his own account, Dictys follows Homer fairly well, although he was one of the first to eliminate the presence of the gods in the actual battle. In his account of the Trojan Horse he eliminates Laocoön and also departs from tradition by having Hector ambushed by Achilles.

A very influential manuscript of the sixth century was a Latin translation of the third-century *History of the Destruction of Troy*, attributed to Dares, and written originally in Greek. Since Latin was better known than Greek, the sixth-century version was widely used as a source by later writers. Like Dictys, Dares begins by claiming that it is the account of an actual person who fought in the Trojan war. However, this character was on the Trojan side, whereas Dictys' narrator was with the Greeks.

Dares goes all the way back to Heracles to begin his story. He has the Greek strong man associated with Jason and the Argonauts. On the way to seek the Golden Fleece, they stop at Troy, where Heracles slays the sea monster to save Hesione and then sacks the city, after being cheated out of his reward (the immortal horses of Zeus) by Laomedon. The story then proceeds through the rebuilding of the city by Priam, and the Judgment of Paris. However, Dares sets an example for numerous writers and artists of the Middle Ages by having the judgment occur in a dream, thus eliminating the actual presence of the goddesses. This is part of his policy to subdue the supernatural element as much as possible.

For the account of the war itself, he follows the *Iliad* generally. In the events that occur after the close of the *Iliad*, Dares simplifies them considerably by completely eliminating the account of the Trojan Horse and the theft of the Palladium, two of the best-known events of the war.

In the ninth century a new twist was introduced to the Trojan legend when Nennius of Wales wrote his *Historia Britonum* in Latin. In this history of Britain, the Welshman, taking a page from

Vergil's *Aeneid,* claimed that Brutus, a son of Ascanius, who was himself a son of Aeneas, settled Britain. The name Britain in this account is a corruption of Brutus.

In the twelfth century Geoffrey of Monmouth, also a Welshman, carried the Trojan-settlement-of-Britain legend still further. But the most enduring new addition to the Trojan saga was made by another twelfth-century writer, Benoît de Sainte-More, who wrote his *Roman de Troie* in French about 1160. Although he drew from both Dares and Ovid, his account contained much new imaginative material.

In keeping with the age of chivalry in which he wrote, as his title indicated, Benoît stressed romance. As a result, his account reflects medieval customs and motivations rather than those of the Greeks of the heroic age. Earlier writers—and later ones as well—had no compunction about distorting history, legend, and Homer. For example, they made up a romance between Achilles and Polyxena (Anonymous, fifth century) and a love affair between Hector and the Amazon queen Penthesilea (Dictys, fourth century). Benoît apparently did not care to distort the Homer canon. In order to get the obligatory romance demanded by the knights and ladies of his time, he invented a completely new one involving Troilus, the son of Priam, and a faithless Trojan girl named Cressida.

In the next century Guido delle Colonne of Sicily made a prose translation in Latin of Benoît de Sainte-More's French verse, but failed to give the Frenchman credit. Latin was more widely read than French in those days, and the tragic story of Troilus and Cressida became more widely known than it had ever been in Benoît's original.

Dante Aligheri (1265–1321) in his *Divine Comedy* used some of the characters of the Trojan legend, but the major contribution to the continuation of the story of Troy was Giovanni Boccaccio's poem, *Il Filostrato,* which further developed the story of Troilus and Cressida. His version, rather than Benoît's, furnished the basic plots for Chaucer's and Shakespeare's stories of the ill-fated Trojan lovers.

Boccaccio also wrote *Genealogia Deorum Gentilium (The*

Genealogy of the Gods) which summarized Greek mythology as taken from the classical writers of antiquity. The book became an important source for future writers on the Troy theme.

Geoffrey Chaucer, author of *The Canterbury Tales,* wrote his *Troilus and Criseyde* in 1382. The story line of the narrative poem follows the basic elements of Benoît's inventions, but is embellished with very effective characterizations and observations of human nature.

Troilus, the son of Priam, is lovesick for Criseyde, a young widow. She is the daughter of Calchas, a Trojan seer, who deserted to the Greeks after his magic assured him that Troy would fall. Pandarus, Criseyde's uncle, acts as go-between to bring Troilus and Criseyde together. Then Calchas persuades the Greeks to exchange a Trojan captive for his daughter Criseyde. Troilus is heartbroken at being thus parted from his love. He and Creseyde pledge their undying love, and he gives her a brooch as a parting gift. Diomedes, a handsome young Greek warrior, is selected to bring Criseyde to the Greek camp.

Criseyde, at their parting, has assured Troilus that she will find a way to slip away and return to him within ten days, but she does not and Troilus sends her a letter. She replies, repledging her love in a rather weak manner. Later in battle Troilus sees the brooch he gave her as a symbol of their love pinned to Diomedes' armor. He knows then that the fickle beauty has given her love to the handsome Greek. His heart broken, Troilus throws himself madly into battle. Several times he seeks to kill Diomedes, but fails each time. Finally he is slain by Achilles.

Chaucer gave his Trojan characters medieval English morals and aspirations. William Shakespeare, in *The History of Troilus and Cressida* (1601), chose to present a picture of the late Renaissance period. For sources he had Chaucer and Robert Henryson (1430–1506), whose *Testament of Cressid* retells Benoît with later inventions. Henryson omits the death of Troilus, picturing him as burying Cressid after she dies of leprosy following her abandonment by Diomedes.

Shakespeare follows Chaucer's story line fairly well, but adds many details and supplementary actions that show his familiarity with the Homeric traditions. However, he early builds up the picture of Cressida as a calculating flirt, whereas Chaucer's Criseyde presents the reader with a surprise at her abrupt change.

We see this in Shakespeare when Pandarus pleads Troilus' case to Cressida. She pretends to be bored by Pandarus' buildup of the young man. But after Pandarus leaves, she soliloquizes that she does find Troilus charming, but that she is not going to rush in, letting him know it.

Shakespeare then shifts the scene to the Achaeans' camp, where Agamemnon is concerned about failing morale. Ulysses (Shakespeare uses the Roman spelling rather than the Greek Odysseus) blames the trouble on Achilles for refusing to fight and on the clowning of Patroclus, of whom the playwright draws a far different picture from Homer's. At this point Aeneas brings them a challenge from Hector for a personal battle between the Trojan champion and one selected from the Greeks.

Achilles is the logical choice, but he is still nursing his wrath. Ulysses then suggests Ajax, who, although a renowned Greek warrior, was born in Troy.

Back in Troy there is a council of war to consider Agamemnon's offer to end the war if Helen is returned to Menelaus. Cassandra, the prophetess daughter of Priam, warns them that Troy will be burned to the ground if the war continues. Hector, heeding her warning, is agreeable to returning Helen, but Troilus and Paris argue that it would be a blot on Trojan honor to give in to the Greeks. Hector, although he knows that the Trojans fought for an evil cause in protecting Helen, agrees that Trojan honor is involved.

Pandarus, to curry favor for himself with the prince of Troy, arranges a tryst between Troilus and Cressida. The two pledge their love. Cressida declares that if she proves false to Troilus, her name will forever be associated with falseness in love. Pandarus then conducts the loving couple to a bedroom.

Meanwhile, Calchas, Cressida's renegade Trojan father, persuades Agamemnon to exchange Antenor, a Trojan prisoner, for Cressida. Diomedes is selected to make the exchange. On the way they pass the tent of Achilles, but scarcely notice him. Achilles is disturbed. As Shakespeare puts it:

ACHILLES.
What, am I poor of late?
'Tis certain, greatness, once fall'n out with fortune
Must fall out with men, too. . . .

Then speaking to Ulysses, he says:

They pass'd by me
As misers do by beggars, neither gave to me
Good word nor look. What, are my deeds forgot?
ULYSSES.
Those scraps are good deeds past, which are devour'd
As fast as they are made, forgot as soon
As done: Perseverance, dear my lord,
Keeps honor bright. . . .

Shakespeare has pointed out in this scene how fleeting fame is. Achilles now realizes that he must return to the fight and do a spectacular act, or all his past glory will be forgotten.

Troilus tries to prevent the exchange of Cressida for Antenor, but cannot persuade Priam. He and Cressida, in a final meeting, pledge eternal love. He mopes in Troy, but Cressida has a different time. She is kissed by all the Greek leaders except Menelaus and Ulysses. She coyly puts off Menelaus, but Ulysses puts *her* off.

ULYSSES.
May I, sweet lady, beg a kiss of you?
CRESSIDA.
You may. [Meaning he could beg]

He replies that he will take the kiss when Helen is a virgin again and back in Menelaus' household. She replies:

> I am your debtor; claim it when 'tis due.
> ULYSSES.
> Never's my day. . .

Later, after Cressida has been taken to her father, Ulysses observes to Nestor:

> ULYSSES.
> Fie, fie upon her!
> There's language in her eye, her cheek, her lip,
> Nay, her foot speaks; her wanton spirits look out
> At every joint and motive of her body.

Ajax and Hector meet in the personal duel, but stop when Hector says he cannot fight a cousin. Ajax agrees and invites Hector, under a truce, to feast with the Greek leaders. At the banquet Achilles, spurred by his injured pride, insults Hector. They agree to fight the following day.

Troilus, who came to the Greek camp with Hector, begs Ulysses to take him to Cressida. He discovers her with Diomedes in a situation that proves that she has already forgotten her Trojan lover. Troilus vows to kill Diomedes.

The next day Hector prepares for battle. Andromaché and Cassandra beg him not to fight, for the signs point to his death. He rejects their appeal. The battle begins, but for some reason best known to the playwright, they do not engage in personal combat as they agreed to do and as Homer shows them. Both fight valiantly, but not with each other. Troilus is unhorsed by Diomedes, who then gives the captured horse to Cressida as a present.

The battle, as is the custom, ends at the close of day. Hector removes his armor when Achilles, accompanied by his Myrmidons, enters.

ACHILLES.

> Look, Hector, how the sun begins to set;
> How ugly night comes breathing at his heels:
> Even with the vail and darking of the sun,
> To close the day up, Hector's life is done.

HECTOR.

> I am unarm'd; forgo this vantage, Greek.

ACHILLES.

> Strike, fellow, strike. This is the man I seek.
>
> [*Hector falls*]
>
> So, Ilion, fall thou next! Now, Troy, sink down!
> Here lies thy heart, thy sinews, and thy bone.
> On, Myrmidons, and cry you all again,
> "Achilles hath the mighty Hector slain."

Troilus carries the word to Troy that Hector is dead and that Achilles is dragging the body about the plain. He meets Pandarus and denounces him as a pander (pimp). The play ends with Pandarus bewailing his fate.

Shakespeare has only a minor role for Helen, but he keeps to tradition in praising her beauty. He has Hector say:

> Is she worth keeping? why, she is a pearl,
> Whose price hath launch'd above a thousand ships. . . .

In this line about launching a thousand ships, Shakespeare echoes Lucian, who originated it, and Christopher Marlowe, who used it to such perfection in *The Tragical History of Dr. Faustus*. Dr. Faustus has signed a pledge with Lucifer, mortgaging his soul to the devil in exchange for twenty-four years of magical gratification of all his desires. As the prescribed time draws to a close, Faustus is talking with some scholars who ask him to conjure up the spirit of Helen so they could see "the admirablest lady that ever liv'd."

Faustus orders Mephostophilus, his demon link with Lucifer, to do so. Helen parades across the stage, and the scholars agree:

No marvel though the angry Greeks pursued
With ten years' war the rape of such a queen
Whose heavenly beauty passeth all compare."

After the scholars leave, Faust, haunted by Helen's beauty, asks the demon to bring her back. . . .

That I might have unto my paramour
That heavenly Helen which I saw of late. . . .

Then, when Helen reenters, Faustus cries:

Was this the face that launch'd a thousand ships,
And burnt the topless towers of Ilium?
Sweet Helen, make me immortal with a kiss!

[*She kisses him.*]

Her lips suck forth my soul: see where it flies!
Come, Helen, come give me my soul again.
Here will I dwell, for heaven is in these lips,
And all is dross that is not Helena.

Of all the lines written about Troy and Helen through the centuries, Marlowe's "Was this the face that launch'd a thousand ships" is probably the best known to the general public. The next is probably Edgar Allan Poe's final two lines of "To Helen."

Helen, thy beauty is to me
Like those Nicean barks of yore,
That gently, o'er a perfumed sea,
The weary, wayworn wanderer bore
To his own native shore.

On desperate seas long wont to roam
Thy hyacinth hair, thy classic face,
Thy Naiad airs have brought me home

> To the glory that was Greece
> And the grandeur that was Rome.

Earlier in the Middle Ages the Trojan legend was spread widely by the enormous popularity of the *Gesta Romanorum*, believed to have been first assembled in the thirteenth century. This was a collection of folk tales with religious morals attached. Where classical scholars never lost their interest in the writings of the ancient authors, the *Gesta* was something the lowest common denominator of the public could understand. Most of them couldn't read, but the *Gesta* was widely quoted orally and used in the lengthy religious sermons of the times.

Tale CLVI (156) tells how a prediction claimed that the Trojan war could not be won without Achilles' being killed in the fighting.

> His mother, fearing this, placed him, in the dress of a female, amongst the ladies of the court of a certain king. Ulixes [Ulysses], suspecting the stratagem, loaded a ship with a variety of wares; and besides the trinkets of women, took with him a splendid suit of armor. Arriving at the castle in which Achilles dwelt among the girls, he exposed his goods for sale. The disguised hero, delighted with the warlike implements upon which he gazed, seized a lance, and gallantly brandished it. The secret was thus manifested, and Ulixes conducted him to Troy.

In England in the seventeenth and eighteenth centuries, chapbooks were popular. These were made of cheap, poorly printed material and were roughly comparable to comic books and paperbacks of today. In them Trojan material was paraphrased in simplified form and was so popular that frequently sequels were written to provide new adventures for the heroes.

The eighteenth and nineteenth centuries produced a mass of material on the Trojan theme. A lot of it was scholarly argument about the authorship of the *Iliad* and the *Odyssey*, about whether Homer really lived and whether the same man wrote both epics. The historical basis of the *Iliad* also came in for considerable argument and speculation.

In the purely literary field, those standing out were Friedrich von Schiller, who in his work *The Victory Feast* tells of the Greek celebration after the war: Johann von Goethe, whose *Faust* loves the shade of Helen (following Marlow), and William Wordsworth, who, in *Laodamia*, provides an account of the wife of the first Greek to die at Troy.

Lord Byron, despite his great love for Greece, never wrote directly about the Trojan war, although he did write a poem praising Canova's bust of Helen. Other English poets who did write about Troy were Alfred Lord Tennyson, Dante Gabriel Rosetti, and William Morris.

In the rush to find different themes for the old story, Samuel Butler came up with a new slant in 1897, when he wrote *The Authoress of the Odyssey*, arguing that only a woman could have written it. This rather fanciful idea was taken up by the modern writer Robert Graves, who wrote *Homer's Daughter* in 1955, a novel that develops Butler's original theme.

Others in the twentieth century include John Erskine's satirical *The Private Life of Helen of Troy* (1925), John Masefield's *A Tale of Troy* (1932), and Jean Giraudoux's *The Tiger at the Gates* (1955).

Inevitably Troy made the motion-picture screen, but not as often as one would have thought. Alexander Korda filmed John Erskine's *The Private Life of Helen of Troy* with Marie Korda, his wife, as Helen. It was released in 1927. Earlier both Vitagraph and Universal are supposed to have made one-reel versions.

In 1956 Warner Brothers released an Italian film, *Helen of Troy*, with Rosanna Podesta as the face that launch'd a thousand ships. The previous year Paramount released *Ulysses*, with Kirk Douglas, which treated the Trojan War only in passing.

None was an outstanding success. Homer had said all there was to say about Troy. All that has come after is, despite varying merit, imitation.

12

TROJAN ART

The art of the early Trojans appears to have been purely utilitarian. In the first Troy, all we have to judge by are a few pots and the fragments of many others. Excavators put great store in pottery, for—as Schliemann wrote—"it is a cornucopia of archaeological wisdom for those dark ages." In the case of the first Troy, we are talking about a time period—allowing for inaccuracies in date—from 3000 to 2500 B.C. The Chinese date the invention of pottery in their realm to the legendary emperor Hwang-ti in 2697 B.C. This would indicate that the Trojans were making pottery at, or well before, this time. W. A. Franks, writing in 1878, observes, "The art of making pottery seems to have been practiced by mankind from very early times. It is even a question whether it was not known to the primitive inhabitants of Europe in those early times when the mammoth and reindeer still lived in the plains of France."

Many of these early handmade Trojan pots were designed with rounded bottoms that prevented them from standing alone. On each side were perforations for hanging, presumably with grass rope. A curious note is that there are double holes on each side. This is very seldom found, although double-holed provisions for hanging have been noted in rare instances in France and Denmark. Schliemann noted that fragments of a pot found in Andalusia, Spain, "in fabric resembles some of the pottery of the first city at Hissarlik."

The original Trojans had already started adding designs to their pottery to enhance their beauty. These were mainly lines in running W's, crosshatches, and herringbone. The color of this pottery was a deep, lustrous black. The luster was achieved by rubbing with polishing stones. The decorations were incised in the wet clay and filled with chalk.

Professor Rudolf Virchow examined the pottery and wrote Schliemann:

> The preparation of the black terra-cotta vessels has in our Berlin Anthropological Society been the subject of many and long discussions. It has been proven that the most common mode of producing them is by slow burning in shut-up places, to produce much smoke, which enters into the clay and impregnates it. The black color can be made of any intensity that is desired.

The Hissarlik vessels have certainly been made in this way.

Another authority expressed the opinion that the black color could have been produced by pine soot.

No trace of painting of any type was found by Schliemann in the first Trojan stratum, but what resembled an owl's face was incised on a piece of bowl. The owl motif was found in increasing numbers in the top layer of Troy I.

Owl-faced idols and bowls were also found extensively in Troy II, along with a more sophisticated pottery. An abundance of gold objects was found. The remarkably artistic work of the golden diadem has previously been described. Along with other smaller jewelry, the Great Treasure, which Schliemann ascribed to Troy II, contained a remarkable double-handled, double-spouted goblet, made of pure gold weighing one pound six ounces troy weight.

A goldsmith consulted by Schliemann gave the opinion that the goblet had been beaten from a single sheet of pure gold. The hollow handles were beaten from two separate pieces of gold and soldered to

A fanciful pot from the Troy VI level still utilizes the owlish face from previous levels. Woodcut from Schliemann's *Ilios*.

the basic cup. The goblet is boat-shaped, measuring 3.6 inches high, 7.5 inches long, and 7.3 inches from handle to handle. The handles are in the center of each side of the bowl. The openings in each end for drinking vary in size. One mouth is 1.4 inches in width. The other is 2.8 inches.

The bowl closely resembles a common gravy boat, but experts have unanimously agreed it was intended for drinking. Schliemann quoted the *Quarterly Review* (1874) to the effect that the goblet was held for drinking with the larger mouth toward the drinker. He could then tip the cup to pour wine from the smaller mouth as a libation to the gods before drinking from the larger mouth himself.

Schliemann called it "one of the most striking and unique objects discovered by me at Troy." The goblet was part of the Great Treasure given to Germany, which disappeared in World War II.

A number of rude plates were discovered in this stratum, proving that the second Trojans had gotten past the stage of eating with their hands from a common bowl. However, experts noted that there were no marks on the plates. This indicated that the Trojans still ate with their hands. Knives would have scratched the partially baked clay.

Another curious object was a rattle made of hollow clay. Two well-sculpted woman's hands hug the globular body. The top terminates in a neck from which the head was broken and lost. Incised marks indicate a necklace around her neck. The body is sealed, but metal particles in the hollow interior produce a rattle when shaken. Schliemann speculated that it was a child's toy, but it could also have been an object used in religious ceremonies and dances.

Another mystery is the meaning of the whorls, as they are called. These terra-cotta disks resemble the whorls used on spindles. They are small disks ranging from an inch to two inches in diameter, thick in the center and tapering to an edge around their circumference. They have a hole through the center and curious inscribed decorations circling both sides.

These decorations, crudely drawn, take all shapes. Although many are similar, none is an exact repetition of another. They range from swastika motifs to stick drawings of stags. Others are curious designs of widely varying shapes. Some of the decorations are surprisingly original in design, although poorly executed.

The crude drawings disturbed Schliemann. Earlier he had found representations of animals and men that were much better executed, and he could not understand why these were so crudely done. He was especially disturbed by some slanting marks he took to represent a man. He said:

> Rude and even horrible as these representations of our species
> are, they are of capital interest. . . . But we have seen that the

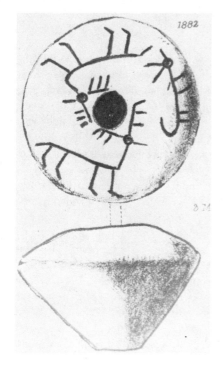

Drawing from Schliemann's *Ilios* shows top and side view of one of the mysterious whorls found in the ruins. The crude figures seem to represent stags and a doe.

Trojans were perfectly capable of modeling in clay tolerably good representations of men and animals. Why then did they incise on their whorls such monstrous figures of men and animals, figures which far exceed in rudeness the rudest drawings of the wild men of Africa?

If we look at the rude but symmetrically shaped pottery, or if we contemplate the masses of gold ornaments which reveal so much artistic skill, and which can only have been the work of a school of artists centuries old—is it possible to suppose that a people so far advanced in civilization could have made such rudest of rude representations of man and animal, unless the latter had been conventional figures, intended as votive offerings to the tutelary deity, figures consecrated by the ages?

In the fourth city we find another curiosity. Pottery apparently grew sex, for there are odd pots with eyes and noses molded into the clay and not just inscribed as before, and with molded breasts jutting out from the sides. The faces still resemble the owlish idols of Troy I, although some are increasingly grotesque. Some of the lids provide curiously peaked hats for the idol pots. Handles on the sides vary greatly. Some are small hoops of clay, designed obviously only for hanging, whereas others are not full loops, but stick up on the sides like sharp horns.

The pottery also shows a stronger tendency to put three tripod legs on the bottom of the pots. A lot of this material shows exceptional ability on the part of the potters.

To the end of the Trojan period we find no painting or statuary beyond fanciful pots and some small terra-cotta figurines. The Hellenistic period of Troy VIII and the Roman Troy IX produced extensive sculpture, judging from reports of travelers. The bronze statues have disappeared, and the marble ones now consist of thousands of fragments, broken up by the early Christians. What remains proves that the statuary was of a high order of art. One found by Schliemann in the Troy VIII stratum is a broken head of a woman with Grecian features who is lovely enough to be a fanciful representation of Helen herself.

From a purely artistic view the best object found in the ruins was a relief of Apollo with four horses of the sun, which came from a temple of the New Ilium period. It is a bold relief, showing the god in flowing robes and spiked helmet standing among the rearing horses.

Heinrich Brunn, an eighteenth-century German art expert, said of it:

As a work of art it shows the greatest skill in solving one of the most difficult of problems: for the team of four horses ought not to move on the surface of the relief, but to appear as if it came out of it at a half-turn. This has been achieved principally by pressing back the right hinder thigh of the horses in the foreground while the left foot steps forward. At the same time the same horse is slightly foreshortened, and the surface of the

Could this be later Troy's conception of Helen? Schliemann found the carving in one of the Trojan layers.

thigh lies deeper than the upper surface of the triglyph. . . . The position of the god is half turned forward, slightly following that of the head. Here also the arm is again slightly turned inward, but not so as to bring the position into conflict with the rules of relief.

If the art of Troy itself is meager, the same cannot be said of art inspired by Troy. From the painted vases of classical Greece to today's masters, artists through the centuries have found inspiration in the various traditions of the famous city and its people.

The first artist to picture a scene of the Trojan war, if Homer can be accounted an accurate recorder, was Helen herself. Just before Helen goes to the Scaean gate to identify the Greeks for Priam, she is visited by the goddess Iris, who has assumed the form of the wife of Antenor's son. Homer relates, "And in the hall she found Helen weaving a great purple web of double fold, and embroidering thereon many battles of horse-taming Trojans and mail-clad Achaeans, that they had endured for her sake at the hands of Ares."

In this forerunner of the great tapestries of the Middle Ages, Helen had an advantage that none of the succeeding artists had: She drew her models from life. Provided, of course, that there was really a Helen, as all of us who love the *Iliad* most fervently hope.

Beginning in the seventh century B.C. and running through all the Greek classical period, Trojan scenes were favorite subjects for vase paintings. They were probably also popular in sculpture, but not much has survived. One example, in the museum at Delphi in Greece, is a frieze carved in the sixth century for one of the treasuries at the Oracle of Apollo.

Although much of this early Trojan art has disappeared long since, both Pausanias and Pliny mention examples that give some idea of the continuing interest. Pausanias mentions the fifth-century artist Polygnotos, who painted two scenes of the fall of Troy. One was in Athens and the other in Delphi. Polygnotos' brother, Aristophon, painted a series of pictures of Heracles and Laomedon, and Helen. Pausanias also mentions Panaeus' painting of Achilles and Penthesilea, work by Phidias and his pupil Agoracritus, Onatas' bronze group of Greek warriors drawing lots to fight Hector, Lycius (son of Myron of the Discobolus fame), who sculpted a number of Iliad characters, and Strongylion, who carved a Trojan horse for the Athens Acropolis.

Pliny lists several famous works of art that stretch over five centuries. One is a Helen painted by Zeuxis, which is supposed to have been modeled by five young beauties, with the artist taking the best features of each to achieve the most beautiful woman of all time. Pliny also mentions Artemon's picture of Heracles and Laomedon, Theorus' painting of Orestes avenging his father Agamemnon, and the "Laocoön" of the sculptors Agesandros, Polydoros, and Athenodorus. (This is the famous marble group in the Vatican.)

The first century A.D. is notable for the superb frescoes and wall paintings later uncovered in the ruins of Pompeii. Just before his death, Schliemann spent many engrossed hours viewing these conceptions of the Troy he loved so dearly.

In the second and third centuries considerable mosaic work was done, depicting Trojan themes. Bronze and marble sculptures were popular. In the fifth century illuminated manuscripts began to appear and continued to do so throughout the Middle Ages. Tapestries were especially popular during this time also.

Raphael, one of the glories of the Renaissance, made designs for Trojan themes, which his students executed in oils, ceramics, and tapestries. The man carrying his aged father and leading his young son by the hand—a detail in Raphael's "Fire in the Borgo"—was said by biographer Vasari (in *Lives of the Artists*) to have been inspired by the Account of Aeneas' escape from Troy.

Lucas Cranach the Elder, the German master, painted the "Judgment of Paris." Like so many painters, Cranach pictured Paris in the costume of the painter's time (1528) and with a Rhine castle representing Troy in the background. In 1601 or thereabout, El Greco (Domenico Theotocopoulos), painted his famous "Laocoön" in the curiously distorted style for which he is famous. El Greco's "Laocoön" is now in the Kress collection in the National Gallery of Art, Washington, D. C.

A contemporary of El Greco was the Flemish master Peter Paul

Rubens, who has a long list of Trojan subjects in museums around the world. He was especially fond of the "Judgment of Paris." Versions of this theme are in the Prado Museum, Madrid, and the National Gallery, Washington. He also did a number dealing with Achilles from his schooling with the centaur to his death.

In the eighteenth century Jean-Antoine Watteau produced a well-known "Judgment of Paris," as did his French colleague, François Boucher, and the German painter, Anton Raphael Mengs. The most prolific painter of Trojan themes in this period was Giovanni Tiepolo. His fresco, "The Sacrifice of Iphigenia," is especially admired. It is in the Villa Valmarana, Vicenza, Italy, and is one of a series depicting scenes from the *Iliad* and the *Odyssey*. He also has a painting on the sacrifice of Iphigenia in the National Gallery, Washington; his "Building of the Trojan Horse" is in the National Gallery, London.

In the nineteenth century Benjamin West, the American painter who built himself a reputation in London, painted "Helen Brought to Paris." Joseph W. M. Turner's "Discord Choosing an Apple in the Garden of the Hesperides" ties in with the Trojan legend, but the remainder of his prolific work is based upon the *Aeneid* rather than Homer. Others of the period are Jacques-Louis David, John Trumbull, William Blake, Jean-Auguste Ingres, Eugene Delacroix, Honoré Daumier, Dante Gabriel Rosetti, Edward Burne-Jones, and Bertel Thorwaldsen, creator of much superb sculpture.

Bridging the nineteenth and twentieth centuries are the sculptor Auguste Rodin and painters Pierre-Auguste Renoir and John Singer Sargent. Picasso, the giant of the twentieth century, only painted one picture with a Trojan tie-in, and this dealt with Ulysses and the sirens on his way home from Troy.

This has been, because of space limitations, only a brief sketch of particularly well-known artists and themes. There are hundreds more—so many that a full book could hardly discuss them all adequately.

13

THE ROAD TO TROY

The ruins of Troy as seen today are not overly impressive when one compares them with the cyclopean walls of Mycenae, the great hall of Knossos, and the grandeur of the Acropolis in Athens. But for all of that, they are intensely interesting and inspiring as one associates each piece of wall or foundation or each piece of broken pottery with some of the most glorious names of literature, mythology, history, archaeology, and art. Troy has plenty to say to students of all these disciplines—and also just to everyday tourists. When a tourist walks through Troy he is retracing the footprints of such renowned tourists as Julius Caesar, Xerxes the Great, Alexander the Great, Pausanias, Antiochus the Great, and even—if we judge by the accuracy of his geographical descriptions of the Troad—Homer.

Although a large number of students and tourists visit Troy each year, surprisingly few Americans can be found among them, despite the number who visit Istanbul. Talking with American tourists in Istanbul, I asked why none of them had included Troy in his itinerary. Most—while they were certainly familiar with the name—were surprised to learn there really was such a place. They considered it either a legend or a totally forgotten spot. Some even asked, "Troy? That's somewhere in Greece, isn't it?"

No, friends, it isn't in Greece. It is four miles inland from the place where the Hellespont opens into the Aegean Sea. The ordinary tours do not include it. The reason is that, though Troy is not difficult to get to, it is off the beaten tourist track. Unfortunately there are no airports near it. The distance is about two hundred miles from Istanbul and about the same from Izmir. To get there, the visitor has the choice of renting a car in Istanbul and driving down the Gallipoli Peninsula to Eceabat, where he crosses the Dardanelles (the Hellespont) on a car ferry to Canakkale, or of taking a bus or ferry from Istanbul.

The bus covers the same route as the car. The water ferry comes down the Sea of Marmara and into the Dardanelles to Canakkale. The boat trip, if one can make schedules, is delightful, but the side trip requires a minimum of two days.

The ferry fare is around ten dollars, and a rented car with driver is about $200. Split among several people, this is not so bad. Its advantage is that one can go to Troy down the historic Gallipoli Peninsula on the European side of the Sea of Marmara and come back up the Asian side to Istanbul.

The drive is pleasant both ways. The road is good blacktop and easy riding, and passes extensive fields of sunflowers and farms along the way. Since the Dardanelles is the water opening to Istanbul, the Gallipoli Peninsula is quite well fortified, and picture taking along the route is not recommended because you never know when you are pointing your camera at some unseen military reservation.

From Canakkale, the Dardanelles crossing point, it is only about six miles to Trova, the modern name for Troy.

As one turns off the Canakkale road on a short spur leading to Trova, the first things visible are two souvenier stands with a three-story wooden horse rising up behind them. The horse was built in 1975, with a small restaurant in its belly and a lookout point on its back where visitors can view the entire ruins.

There is a small museum at the entrance, but the only items on display are some later-period pots. All the good articles have been removed to the Trojan Museum in Canakkale or to the National

Museum in Istanbul. The Great Treasure that Schliemann stole and gave to Germany before his death was lost when the Russians took Berlin in 1945. It is not known whether the golden objects were taken back to Russia, hidden by Germans, or stolen by German or Russian troops.

A fence surrounds the ruins area and a small admission charge is required to get in. Guidebooks are available in English, and an English-speaking guide, who is thoroughly versed on the ruins and their history, is available for about two dollars. He can even draw you a map in the dirt that is better than what you'll see in the guidebooks.

You enter the actual ruins at the east gate of Troy, which are the remains of Troy VI. The route then takes you past Schliemann's Great Ditch, where the walls of Troy I houses are visible, and on up the hill there the temple of Athena once sat.

When you come to the remains of the outer wall, you can look out over the Troad, but cannot see either the Aegean Sea or the Hellespont. Both are hidden by low hills in the distance. The local peasants can be seen in the summer as they work in the fields, recalling to the visitor Homer's statement about the wheat fields running up to the Trojan walls.

A particularly interesting portion is the ramped road leading up to what was once the gate of Troy II. It is a steep incline paved with flagstones. Other interesting sites are the mound of the megaron of Troy II, the great house in which the king of Troy lived, the "pillar house" of Troy VI, the sacrificial altar, just outside the wall of Troy VI, used by the Greeks of Troy VIII, and the small marble-seated theater of the Roman Troy IX.

Schliemann in his frantic quest for treasure left little of the small remains of Homer's Troy. We can see a portion of wall and one house foundation attributed to Troy VII-a. It shows large jugs sunk in the floor for storage of grain. The tops were sealed with stone slabs. The necessity for storing provisions underground indicates the crowded nature of the citadel during this period and the need to keep a large amount of provisions inside the wall as a protection against starvation during a siege.

Entrance to the ruins themselves is through the remains of the east gate of Troy VI. Parts of these walls not destroyed by the earthquake were used for Troy VII-a, Homer's Ilium.

Troy is not an extensive ruin. A couple of hours is more than sufficient for an ordinary tourist visit. Visitors interested in archaeology may want to spent anywhere from a day to a week studying the different strata left revealed by the excavations.

As an archaeological site, Troy is considered worked out. It is not completely excavated, but further work is not possible without destroying the important remains of different layers. Even the possibility of finding another treasure or other important discoveries does not make this worthwhile. Valuable work might be done in surrounding areas to determine the extent of Trojan influence in its time, but no one has been interested enough to put up the money. Many areas that might be fruitful for archaeological exploration are closed military ranges.

The smallness of the Trojan remains makes a trip directly to Troy a rather small reward for such a long journey. It is best seen as part of a Homeric tour, which includes Greece. This would involve a visit to the beautiful ruins of Delphi and the cyclopean walls of Mycenae. Mycenae can be seen in a single day's bus trip from Athens. This is an excursion that goes to Old Corinth, where Saint Paul preached, and then to Mycenae and Epidaraus, which has the best-preserved of the old Greek theaters.

Going into Mycenae, the visitors stop at the so-called tomb of Atreus, Agamemnon's father. This is a tremendous beehive-shaped stone structure of great interest. From its approach one can look across the valley where Mycenae is located on the top of hill.

From a purely tourist viewpoint, Mycenae is more interesting than Troy. As the visitor approaches, he sees the tremendous walls, which well earn their reputation of having been built by Cyclops. The entrance is through the famed Lion Gate with its relief of two rampant lions. Directly inside the gate is the circle of stones around the shaft graves where Schliemann uncovered the golden mask he incorrectly attributed to Agamemnon. The trail then leads upward to the ruins on the city's acropolis. There is a beautiful view across the olive orchards and farms on the Plain of Argos.

Back in Athens the museums contain important relics of Mycenae, and it may be possible to visit the home of Schliemann.

Then from Athens the route is across the Aegean to Turkey. There is a four-day boat tour from Athens that takes in important points in Ionia, such as Ephesus, but does not reach Troy. A one-day flight tour from Athens enables one to see Knossos in Crete, the home of the Mycenaean culture.

In Turkey the gateway to Troy is Istanbul, a magnificent city jammed with historical relics of the great Byzantine Empire and the Crusades. The half-day tour from Istanbul by ferry up the Bosporus

The cylopean walls of Mycenae, built on naked rock, formed the stronghold of Agamemnon, who led the Greeks in the Trojan War.

to the Black Sea and back along the coast by bus is worth the price of the entire trip. In Istanbul there is the Topkapi, formerly a seraglio but now a museum, St. Sophia, the Blue Mosque, the Golden Horn with its tangle of ships, and the Roman Hippodrome, among hundreds of other sights.

Aside from Istanbul and Troy, visitors will find Turkey a fabulous land where every location seems to have a historical association. There is Gordium, near Ankara, where Alexander cut the Gordian Knot, Goreme with its strange natural formations, Sardis with its associations of Croesus, Aesop, and Solon, the fortress Rumeli Hisar from which Mehmet directed the fall of Constantinople, and many others.

All of this, combined with the associations of Homer, makes a trip to Troy a wonderful excursion into ancient history. All that is missing is Helen herself, and her stand-in shows up in August when a local girl in ancient costume personifies the "face that launch'd a thousand ships" at a festival held at the ruins.

CHRONOLOGY

Authorities do not agree on the precise dating of prehistory and early history. Dates are subject to revision in the light of continuing scholarship. This chronology lists major known dates in the history of Troy, along with corresponding world-history dates for comparative purposes.

3000 B.C. Founding of Troy I

2500 B.C. Destruction of Troy I

2500–2200 B.C. Time of Troy II

2200–2050 B.C. Time of Troy III

2050–1900 B.C. Time of Troy IV

1900–1800 B.C. Time of Troy V

1800–1300 B.C. Time of Troy VI

1300–1260 B.C. Time of Troy VII-a*

1270–1260 B.C. Estimated time of Homer's Trojan War.*

1260–1190 B.C. Time of Troy VII-b $_1$

1190–1100 B.C. Time of Troy VII-b $_2$

1100–900 B.C. Unknown period in Troy

900–350 B.C. Time of Troy VIII

3100 B.C. Two kingdoms of Egypt united under Menes.

2575 (c) B.C. Construction of the Great Pyramid of Egypt

2100 B.C. Construction of the ziggurat of Ur of the Chaldees

2000 B.C. Mycenaeans invade Greece

1900 B.C. Hittites invade Anatolia

1750 B.C. Time of Hammurabi. Golden age of Crete

1304 B.C. Beginning of reign of Ramses II

1240 B.C. One reputed date of the Hebrew Exodus from Egypt under leadership of Moses

1150 B.C. Beginning of Dorian invasions that ended Mycenaean empire

1000 B.C. Rise of Sidon and Tyre

775 B.C. Possible time of Homer

753 B.C. Founding of Rome

*Dates controversial.

181

480 B.C. Xerxes visits Troy

350 B.C. Building of Troy IX

334 B.C. Alexander the Great visits Troy

85 B.C. New Ilium attacked by the rebel, Fimbria

46 B.C. Caesar interested in Troy

25 B.C. Augustus considers Troy as possible Roman capital

480 B.C. Battle of Salamis ends Persian invasion of Greece

332 B.C. Alexander conquers Egypt

85 B.C. Rome wars with Mithridates

44 B.C. Death of Julius Caesar

27–14 B.C. Reign of Augustus

A.D.

43 Nero lauds Troy in speech

214 Caracalla at Troy

354 Temples open at New Ilium but city dispersed

400 Apparent abandonment of Trojan site

400–1588 Site of Troy forgotten

1588 Pietro Beloni visits Troad, seeking site of Troy

1786 Le Chevalier places site of Troy at Bunarbashi

1822 Birth of Schliemann

1868 Schliemann excavates Bunarbashi

1870 Schliemann begins excavating at Hissarlik.

1873 Discovery of the Great Treasure

1876 Schliemann discovers treasure of Mycenae

1890 Schliemann dies in Italy

1893–1894 Dörpfeld continues excavations at Troy

1894–1932 Excavations at Troy dormant

1932–1936 Cincinnati Expedition excavates at Hissarlik

1936 Troy open to tourists

A.D.

211–217 Caracalla reigns in Rome

324 Imperial edict forbids worship of ancient gods

1565 Founding of St. Augustine, oldest city in the United States

1588 England defeats Spanish Armada

1788 U.S. Constitution ratified

1824 John Quincy Adams elected President of United States

1869 Completion of transcontinental railroad in the United States

1876 United States celebrates centennial

BIBLIOGRAPHY

Aksit, Ilhan, A *Guide to Troy*. Istanbul: Matbassi, not dated.

Blegen, Carl, *Troy and the Trojans*. N.Y.: Frederick A. Praeger, 1963.

Gesta Romanorum, edited by Swan, Charles and Wynnard Hooper. London: Bohm Library, 1876.

Homer, *The Iliad*. Edited by Leaf, Lang, Myers. London: Macmillan, 1882.

————, *The Odyssey*. Edited by G. H. Palmer. Baltimore: Penguin Books, 1951.

Kitto, H. D. F., *The Greeks*. Baltimore: Penguin Books, 1951.

Lang, Andrew, *Homer and His Age*. London: Longmans, Green, 1906.

Leaf, Walter, *Homer and History*. London: Macmillan, 1915.

Lucian, *Selected Satires*. Edited by L. Casson. Garden City: Doubleday, 1962.

Lucian, *True History*. Translated by P. Turner. Bloomington: Indiana U. Press, 1958.

Marlowe, Christopher, *Tragical History of Dr. Faustus*. London: Metheun & Co., 1932.

Payne, Robert, *The Gold of Troy*. N.Y.: Funk and Wagnalls, 1959.

Schliemann, Heinrich, *Ilios: the City and Country of the Trojans*. New York: Harper & Bros., 1880.

————, *Mycenae: A Narrative of Researches and Discoveries*. N.Y.: Scribner, Armstrong & Co., 1878.

Schuchhardt, Karl, *Schliemann's Excavations*. London: Mcmillan & Co., 1891.

Shakespeare, William, *Troilus and Cressida*. N.Y.: Macmillan Publishing Co., 1967.

INDEX

184